MW00699260

A Prayer Book
of Eucharistic
Adoration

A Prayer Book
of Eucharistic
Adoration

Compiled by
William G. Storey
University of Notre Dame

LOYOLA PRESS.
A JESUIT MINISTRY
Chicago

LOYOLAPRESS.
A JESUIT MINISTRY

3441 N. Ashland Avenue
Chicago, Illinois 60657
(800) 621-1008
www.loyolapress.com

In accordance with c. 827, permission to publish is granted on June 11, 2010 by Very
Reverend John F. Canary, Vicar General of the Archdiocese of Chicago. Permission
to publish is an official declaration of ecclesiastical authority that the material is
free from doctrinal and moral error. No legal responsibility is assumed by the grant
of this permission.

Copyright acknowledgments appear on pages 292–295 and constitute a continuation of
this copyright page.

Library of Congress Cataloging-in-Publication Data
Storey, William George, 1923-
  Eucharistic adoration / William G. Storey.
    p. cm.
  ISBN-13: 978-0-8294-2906-0
  ISBN-10: 0-8294-2906-9
  1. Lord's Supper--Adoration. 2. Spiritual life--Catholic Church. 3. Catholic
Church--Liturgy. I. Title.
  BX2233.S76 2010
  264'.02036--dc22

                                                                2010011401

Printed in China
10 11 12 13 14 15 16 RRD/China 10 9 8 7 6 5 4 3 2 1

This book is dedicated to those devout Catholics who engage in adoration of the Blessed Sacrament in our churches.

Contents

Part 4: Novenas and Triduums of Intercessory Prayer

Part 6: Devotions to the Blessed Virgin Mary

Part 7: The Rosary before the Blessed Sacrament

Preface

My father was indifferent to religion, but my mother raised me as a member of the Anglican Church. I came to love the Book of Common Prayer of the Church of England in Canada and entered wholeheartedly into its liturgy, and especially its Holy Eucharist. But as I grew into my teen years I discovered that my experience of "prayer book" religion was remarkably different from that of many of my fellow parishioners and even of my rector's.

As an altar boy of seventeen I was serving a visiting Anglican priest one Sunday when I made a shattering discovery. As I was putting out the candles I noticed that a fair amount of the Communion bread and consecrated wine remained on the altar. I drew the priest's attention to this and got this answer: "Well, throw the bread out to the birds and pour the wine back into the bottle."

In shock I reported these remarks to my rector and his reply proved even more disconcerting. Without turning a hair he told me that some priests believed in the Real Presence of Jesus in Holy Communion and others did not. "And you will just have to get used to it!" A cold moment for me, if there ever was one!

I made a change. My maternal grandmother was a Catholic and I started visiting her church after school to pray before the Blessed Sacrament. One day as I was leaving Our Lady of Mercy a young priest stopped me and asked if I was a parishioner. When I told him

I wasn't, he asked what I was doing in their church. I told him I was making a visit to the Blessed Sacrament. That began a brief conversation about my religious condition and an invitation to visit the parish house some time.

When I knocked at that door a few weeks later, the rather older pastor answered it and after a few preliminaries asked if I would like to be taken through the catechism. I did, and soon discovered that Catholics did indeed believe in the Real Presence and that it was not optional.

At the end of our course in the catechism, I hesitated to commit myself to the Catholic Church. At the pastor's urging me to "pray about it," I decided to make a Holy Hour before the tabernacle each day for a month. For the month of May I prayed before the Blessed Sacrament with the book *Visits to the Blessed Sacrament and to the Virgin Mary* by St. Alphonsus de Liguori. The result? I was conditionally baptized on May 31 and received my first Holy Communion on June 1, the feast of Pentecost.

Eucharistic prayer was crucial to my becoming a Catholic. Now you know why I am more than delighted to put together a prayer book of Eucharistic devotions.

Blessed be Jesus in the most Holy Sacrament of the Altar!

William G. Storey

Introduction

Primarily this book is for devout Catholics who want to spend time in adoration before Jesus in the tabernacle. And yet, we begin with the Mass, the supreme realization of the Eucharist, then prayers before and after Holy Communion, and brief visits to the Blessed Sacrament.

A passage from a book on the fullness of the Eucharistic reality helps us to understand how adoration of the Presence is related and subordinate to the Mass:

> *It is true that eucharistic devotions are derivative from the Mass; they developed in the Middle Ages, rather late in the Church's history, and even now the directives the Church gives for them clearly make them subordinate to the eucharistic celebration. The Blessed Sacrament always points back to the Mass and always retains the sense of food that the bread and wine of the liturgy possess; the sacrament is there ultimately to be consumed and to nourish us. Still, it has developed its own spirituality as a variation on that of the Mass itself. A study of eucharistic presence that omitted any discussion of devotion to the Blessed Sacrament would be incomplete.*[1]

Therefore, the adoration section of the prayer book follows the section on the Mass and Holy Communion.

We begin with brief prayers before the reserved sacrament. A larger and much more expressive seven-day set of visits to our Lord in the tabernacle takes up many pages. Then there follows an Office of the Blessed Sacrament that may be prayed in part or in whole by a single person, by two people, or by a group of adorers led by a leader.

Then there are seven holy hours before the tabernacle: one dedicated to the Blessed Sacrament and the other to the Sacred Heart of Jesus; then five holy hours for the special seasons of the church year: Advent, Christmastide, Lent, Holy Week, and Eastertide.

The next section contains four novenas and triduums of prayer that we need to express ourselves before God, personally and in families and other groups: in honor of the Blessed Sacrament, to the five wounds of Jesus, to the Sacred Heart of Jesus, and to his Precious Blood. There follows a description of the special days in honor of the Eucharist: the Forty Hours devotion in every diocese each year, the Holy Thursday observance before the altar of reserve, and the processions and other forms of devotion on the solemnity of Corpus Christi.

Then there is a broad selection of litanies of intercession for individuals, families, and groups of adorers in church. These are rich and varied expressions of our faith that set us properly and emphatically before the Eucharistic Lord in his holy house. One of the first emphases of Eucharistic Adoration were forms of intercessory prayer—especially litanies—and they just as useful now.

Finally, there are two major forms of devotion to our Lady of the Blessed Sacrament: first, a helpful collection of traditional prayers to Mary, and then another dedicated to the Rosary before the Tabernacle, one of the most beneficial forms of prayer, combining both meditation on the chief mysteries of Christ's life and an expressive Marian devotion that supports and favors Mary's role in the divine economy.

It's the Mass that Matters

The Holy Eucharist is the very center and summit of the Catholic liturgy. The Lord's Supper on the Lord's Day is the height of the Christian week and the heart of the Church's worship. It is in Word and Sacrament that we encounter the Christ who teaches, inspires, transforms, and unites us more and more surely to himself and to the Christian community of believers. The fact of our Sunday Mass is what marks us as Catholic Christians and establishes us at the heart of the Communion of Saints.

> "Christ has died, Christ is risen,
> Christ will come again."

> "The Eucharist, as Christ's saving presence in the community of the faithful and its spiritual food, is the most precious possession which the Church can have in her journey through history."
> **Pope John Paul II (1920–2005)[2]**

All the prayers and readings necessary for the celebration of the Mass are contained in the reformed Roman Missal of 1970. Thanks to the Second Vatican Council and its fine liturgical work, the Missal embodies the fullness of our Eucharistic tradition and renders it in our own language for our fuller understanding and celebration. This Missal also provides for Holy Communion under the forms of both bread and wine so that by receiving both we can appreciate on a deeper level Christ crucified for us and for our salvation: "Take and eat, this is my Body; take and drink, this is my Blood."

Outside Sundays and feasts of obligation, the principal sign of our devotion to the Eucharist is attendance at daily Mass. The thirst for the divine mysteries expresses itself across the Catholic world in this manner and reveals our deep desire to satiate ourselves with the body and blood of our Savior.

In addition, thanks to the practice of reserving the Blessed Sacrament for the sick and dying, everywhere in the world Catholics can be seen at prayer in our churches outside of any liturgical celebration. The very center of such prayer is the Blessed Sacrament reserved in the tabernacle; it is the repository of the true, real, and substantial body and blood, soul and divinity of Jesus Christ, the focus of adoration for millions of believers across the centuries, even unto the end of time.

Five Foundational Texts of Our Liturgy

To uncover the sources of our tradition of faith and encourage us to see deeper into the theology and practice of Eucharistic piety, let us begin with five texts from our ancient tradition.

The first of these is Saint Paul the Apostle's teaching on the Lord's Supper; then there follows two very early descriptions of the celebration of the Holy Eucharist from the late first and the mid-second century; then there is a brief quotation from a eucharistic homily by Saint Thomas Aquinas, the prince of theologians, and finally, a hymn by Aquinas, the author of the Mass and

Office of Corpus Christi, the culminating form of the Church's teaching and worship on the Holy Eucharist.

The First Account of the Eucharist: Saint Paul, Before 65 AD

Flee from the worship of idols. I speak as to sensible people; judge for yourselves what I say. The cup of blessing that we bless, is it not a sharing in the blood of Christ? Because there is one bread, we who are many are one body, for we all partake of the one bread. . . . I do not want you to be partners with demons. You cannot drink of the cup of the Lord and the cup of demons. You cannot partake of the table of the Lord and the table of demons. . . .

For I received from the Lord what I also handed on to you, that the Lord Jesus on the night when he was betrayed took a loaf of bread, and when he had given thanks, he broke it and said, "This is my body that is broken for you. Do this in remembrance of me." In the same way he took the cup also, after supper, saying, "This cup is the new covenant in my blood. Do this, as often as you drink it, in remembrance of me." For as often as you eat this bread and drink the cup, you proclaim the Lord's death until he comes. Whoever, therefore, eats the bread or drinks the cup of the Lord in an unworthy manner will be answerable for the body and blood of the Lord. Examine yourselves, and only then eat of bread and drink of the cup. For all who eat or drink in an unworthy manner without discerning the body, eat and drink judgment against themselves.

Saint Paul the Apostle,
I Corinthians 10:14–21; 11:23–29, ca. 52 AD

Another Very Early Account:
Late First Century

On the Lord's Day, you should assemble, break bread, and celebrate the Eucharist, but first having confessed your transgressions, in order that your sacrifice may be untainted. No one who has had a quarrel with a fellow Christian should join your assembly until they have made up, so that your sacrifice may not be defiled. For this is what the Lord meant when he said: "At every place and time offer me a clean sacrifice, for I am a great king, says the Lord, and my name is wonderful among the heathen" (Malachi 1:11, 14).

The Didache[3]

A Second-Century Account of
Sunday Mass

On the day called Sunday there is a meeting in one place of those who live in cities or the country, and the memoirs of the apostles or the writings of the prophets are read as long as time permits. When the reader has finished, the president in a discourse urges and invites [us] to the imitation of these noble things. Then we all stand up together and offer prayers. When we have finished the prayer, bread is brought, and wine and water, and the president similarly sends up prayers and thanksgiving to the best of his ability, the congregation assents, saying its Amen; the distribution and reception of the consecrated elements by each one, takes place and they are sent to the absent by the deacons . . .

We all hold this common gathering on Sunday, since it is the first day [of the week], on which God transforming darkness and matter made the universe, and Jesus Christ our Savior rose from the dead on the same day.

Justin Martyr (ca. 100–ca. 165)[4]

St. Thomas Aquinas:
The Greatest of Miracles

No other sacrament can be more wholesome. By it sins are purged away; virtues are increased; and the soul is enriched with an abundance of every spiritual gift. The Church offers it for both the living and the dead so that what was instituted for all might be to the advantage of all. We cannot fully express the attractiveness of this sacrament in which we taste spiritual delight at its source and in which we renew the surpassing love which Christ revealed to us in his passion. In order to impress the immensity of his love for us, at the last supper, while celebrating the Passover Meal with his disciples, Jesus instituted this sacrament as a perpetual memorial of his passion, as the fulfillment of all the Old Testament types, as the greatest of his miracles, and as a unique consolation for his physical absence.

St. Thomas Aquinas, OP (1225–1274)[5]

A Eucharistic Hymn of
St. Thomas Aquinas

This hymn was composed by Saint Thomas Aquinas for the new feast of the Body and Blood of Christ (Corpus Christi) that was extended to the universal church by Pope Urban IV in 1264. This marvelous hymn became a theologically valuable contribution for the Mass and Office of that feast: it is sung at Vespers to both open and close the feast day and during the sacramental processions that are held outside of church on that occasion. At Benediction of the Blessed Sacrament, the last two stanzas of this famous hymn (*Tantum ergo*) are sung just before the giving of the blessing.

The profound Eucharistic theology contained in this hymn expresses the dogma of transubstantiation in a form of poetic hymnody available to all. Thomas enshrined this beautiful and powerful hymn at the heart of both the Eucharistic celebration and of our personal piety before the tabernacle.

Hail our Savior's glorious Body,
Which his Virgin Mother bore;
Hail the Blood, which shed for sinners,
Did a broken world restore.
Hail the sacrament most holy,
Flesh and Blood of Christ adore!

To the Virgin, for our healing,
His own Son the Father sends;
From the Father's love proceeding
Sower, seed, and Word descends;
Wondrous life of Word incarnate
With his greatest wonder ends!

On that paschal evening see him
With the chosen twelve recline,
To the old law still obedient
In its feast of love divine;
Love divine the new law giving,
Gives himself as Bread and Wine!

By his word the Word almighty
Makes of bread his flesh indeed;

Wine becomes his very life-blood:
Faith God's living Word must heed!
Faith alone may safely guide us
Where the senses cannot lead!

Come, adore this wondrous presence;
Bow to Christ, the source of grace!
Here is kept the ancient promise
Of God's earthly dwelling place!
Sight is blind before God's glory,
Faith alone may see his face!

Glory be to God the Father,
Praise to his co-equal Son,
Adoration to the Spirit,
Bond of love, in Godhead one!
Blest be God by all creation
Joyously while ages run!

St. Thomas Aquinas, OP (1225–1274)[6]

With these traditional texts in mind, let us examine and use the variety of expressions of the Eucharist in the life of the Church and how they can glorify God and spiritually enrich our lives.

Part 1
Mass and Holy Communion

By its very name the Eucharist is the Great Thanksgiving by which we express our profound gratitude for our creation and redemption in Christ our Lord. Over the centuries private forms of preparation and thanksgiving to declare and embody our appreciation for the reception of Holy Communion have emerged, and supplementary devotions to the Mass have grown up to express our adoration for the Real Presence.

The theological point of all this is the Catholic doctrine on transubstantiation that embodies the permanently valid teaching of the famous Council of Trent (1545–1563): "After the consecration of the bread and wine, our Lord Jesus Christ, true God and true man, is truly, really, and substantially contained in the august sacrament of the Holy Eucharist under the appearance of these sensible things [bread and wine]."[7] This teaching is a mystery of faith that surpasses all human understanding and can only be taken on faith.

The prayers presented here are customary before and after Holy Communion, at home, or in church. A good preparation guarantees a good Holy Communion and a good Holy Communion inspires a fervent thanksgiving for the gift of the Eucharist.

Prayers Before Mass and Holy Communion

Blessed Angela of Foligno (ca. 1248–1309), one of the most famous Franciscan mystics of the thirteenth century, tells us why we go to Mass and receive Holy Communion.

> *Why should I go to this mystery [of the Eucharist]? I will tell you what I think. One should go to receive in order to be received, go pure in order to be purified, go alive in order to be enlivened, go just in order to be justified, go united and conjoined to Christ in order to be incorporated through him, with him, and in him, God uncreated and God made man, who is given in this most holy and most high mystery, through the hands of the priest. Thanks be to God always. Amen.*

Blessed Angela of Foligno (ca. 1248–1309)[8]

What do we intend to do when we attend Mass? This intention is set forth for us in the Roman Missal.

My Intention Before Mass

I intend to celebrate Mass
in union with my parish priest,
to receive the body and blood of our Lord Jesus
    Christ
according to the rite of the holy Roman Church
to the praise of our all-powerful God

and all his assembly in the glory of heaven,
for my good and of all the good of the pilgrim
    Church on earth,
and for all who have asked me to pray for them
in general and in particular,
and for the good of the holy Roman Church.

May the almighty and merciful Lord
grant us joy and peace,
amendment of life,
room for true repentance,
the grace and comfort of the Holy Spirit,
and perseverance in good works. Amen.[9]

Receiving the Eucharistic body and blood of our Lord is
the closest we shall come to Jesus in this life. Prayers
before and after Communion stir up our hearts to
appreciate and assimilate the divine gift.

Preface of Corpus Christi

Father, all-powerful and ever-living God,
we do well always and everywhere to give you
    thanks
through Jesus Christ our Lord.

At the last supper,
as he sat at the table with the apostles,
he offered himself to you as the spotless Lamb,
the acceptable gift that gives you perfect praise.
Christ has given us this memorial of his passion
to bring us its saving power until the end of time.

In this great sacrament you feed your people
and strengthen them in holiness,
so that the family of mankind
may come to walk in the light of one faith,
in one communion of love.
We come then to this wonderful sacrament
to be fed at your table
and grow into the likeness of the risen Christ.

Roman Missal, from the preface of Corpus Christi[10]

A Eucharistic Offering

Lord, all things in heaven and earth are yours.
I desire to offer myself to you
in free and perpetual oblation,
so that I may forever be with you.
Lord, in simplicity of heart,
I offer myself this day to you,
to be your servant in service and sacrifice
    of perpetual praise.
Accept me with the oblation of your precious
    body,
which this day I offer you in the presence
of your holy angels, here invisibly present,
so that it may be to my salvation
and to the salvation of all people.

Thomas à Kempis (ca. 1380–1471)[11]

Sancti Venite

This ancient Irish prayer is the epitome of Celtic devotion.

Draw near and take the body of the Lord,
and drink the holy blood for you outpoured.
Saved by that body and that holy blood,
with souls refreshed, we render thanks to God.
Humanity is ransomed from eternal loss
by flesh and blood offered upon the cross.
Salvation's giver, Christ, the only Son,
by his dear cross and blood the victory won.
Offered was he for greatest and for least,
himself the victim, and himself the priest.
Victims were offered by the law of old,
which in a type this heavenly mystery told.
He, Ransomer from death, and light from shade,
now gives his holy grace his saints to aid.
Approach him then with faithful hearts sincere,
and take the safeguard of salvation here.
He, that his saints in this world rules and shields,
to all believers life eternal yields;
With heavenly bread makes them that hunger
      whole,
gives living waters to the thirsting soul. Amen.[12]

Saint Anselm of Canterbury: Preparation Prayer

Saint Anselm was a foremost philosopher and theologian but also contributed to medieval piety by writing various prayers to saints and especially this prayer of preparation for Holy Communion.

Lord Jesus Christ,
by the Father's plan and by the working
   of the Holy Spirit
of your own free will you died
and mercifully redeemed the world
from sin and everlasting death.
I adore and venerate you
as much as ever I can,
though my love is so cold, my devotion so poor.
Thank you for the good gift
of this your holy Body and Blood,
which I desire to receive, as cleansing from sin,
and for a defense against it.

Lord, I acknowledge that I am far from worthy
to approach and touch this sacrament;
but I trust in that mercy
which caused you to lay down your life for sinners
that they might be justified
and because you gave yourself willingly
as a holy sacrifice to the Father.
A sinner, I presume to receive these gifts
so that I may be justified by them.
I beg and pray you, therefore, merciful lover of us all,

let not that which you have given for the cleansing
of sins
be unto the increase of sin,
but rather for forgiveness and protection.

Make me, O Lord, so to perceive with lips and
heart
and know by faith and love,
that by virtue of this sacrament I may deserve
to be
planted in the likeness of your death and
resurrection
by mortifying the old man,
and by the renewal of the life of righteousness.
May I be worthy to be incorporated into your
body
"which is the church,"
so that I may be your member and you may be my
head,
and that I may remain in you and you in me.
Then at the Resurrection you will refashion
the body of my humiliation
according to the body of your glory,
as you promised by your holy apostle,
and I shall rejoice in you for ever
to your glory
who with the Father and the Holy Spirit
lives and reigns for ever. Amen.

St. Anselm of Canterbury (ca. 1033–1109)[13]

A Preparation Prayer of St. Thomas Aquinas

St. Thomas Aquinas, the great theologian, wrote two important prayers for before and after Holy Communion.

Almighty and ever-living God,
I approach the sacrament of your only-begotten
    Son,
      our Lord Jesus Christ.
I come sick to the doctor of life,
unclean to the fountain of mercy,
blind to the radiance of eternal light,
poor and needy to the Lord of heaven and earth.

Lord, in your great generosity,
heal my sickness, wash away my defilement,
enlighten my blindness, enrich my poverty,
and clothe my nakedness.

May I receive the bread of angels,
the King of kings and Lord of lords,
with humble reverence,
with the purity and faith,
the repentance and love,
and the determined purpose
that will help to bring me to eternal salvation.
May I receive the sacrament of the Lord's body
    and blood,
and its reality and power.

Kind God,
may I receive the body of your only-begotten Son

our Lord Jesus Christ,
from the womb of the Virgin Mary,
and so be received into his mystical body
and numbered among his members.

Loving Father,
as on my earthly pilgrimage
I now receive your beloved Son
under the veil of a sacrament,
may I one day see him face to face in glory,
who lives and reigns with you for ever. Amen.

Attributed to St. Thomas Aquinas (1225–1274)[14]

A Eucharistic Hymn of St. Thomas Aquinas

Hidden here before me, Lord, I worship you,
Hidden in these symbols, yet completely true.
Lord, my soul surrenders, longing to obey,
And in contemplation wholly faints away.

Seeing, touching, tasting: these are all deceived;
Only through the hearing can it be believed.
Nothing is more certain: Christ has told me so;
What the truth has uttered, I believe and know.

Only God was hidden when you came to die:
Human nature also here escapes the eye.
Both are my profession, both are my belief:
Bring me to the Kingdom, like the dying thief.

I am not like Thomas, who could see and touch;
Though your wounds are hidden, I believe as
    much.

Let me say so boldly, meaning what I say,
Loving you and trusting, now and every day.

Record of the Passion, when the Lamb was slain,
Living bread that brings us back to life again:
Feed me with your presence, make me live on you;
Let that lovely fragrance fill me through and
      through.

Once a nesting pelican gashed herself to blood
For the preservation of her starving brood:
Now heal me with your blood, take away my guilt:
All the world is ransomed if one drop is spilt.

Jesus, for the present seen as through a mask,
Give me what I thirst for, give me what I ask:
Let me see your glory in a blaze of light,
And instead of blindness give me, Lord, my sight.
    Amen.

Adoro Te devote,
attributed to St. Thomas Aquinas (1225–1274)[15]

Prayers of Thanksgiving
after Communion

> The precious time of thanksgiving after communion should not be neglected: besides the singing of an appropriate hymn it can be most helpful to remain in recollected silence.
> **Pope Benedict XVI**, *Sacramentum Caritatis*, # 50

Aquinas's Thanksgiving after Communion

Lord, Father all-powerful and ever-living God,
I thank you,
for even though I am a sinner,
and your unprofitable servant,
you have fed me
with the precious body and blood of your Son,
    our Lord Jesus Christ,
not because of my worth but out of your kindness
    and your mercy.

I pray that this holy communion
may not bring me condemnation and punishment
but forgiveness and salvation.
May it be a helmet of faith
and a shield of good will.
May it purify me from evil ways
and put an end to my evil passions.
May it bring me charity and patience,
humility and obedience,

and growth in the power to do good.
May it be my strong defense
against all my enemies, visible and invisible,
and the perfect calming of all my evil impulses,
bodily and spiritual.
May it unite me more closely to you,
the one true God,
and lead me safely through death
to everlasting happiness with you.

And I pray that you will lead me, a sinner,
to the banquet where you,
with your Son and the Holy Spirit,
are true and perfect light,
total fulfillment, everlasting joy,
and perfect happiness to your saints.
Grant this through Christ our Lord.
Amen.

Attributed to St. Thomas Aquinas (1225–1274)[16]

Jesus Help Me
John Hardon, SJ, an American Jesuit spiritual director,
is well known for this affective prayer.

Jesus, help me, your servant,
whom you redeemed by your precious blood:

In every need let me come to you with humble
        trust, saying,
~JESUS, HELP ME.
In all my doubts, perplexities, and temptations,
~JESUS, HELP ME.

In hours of loneliness, weariness, and trial,
~JESUS, HELP ME.
In the failure of my plans and hopes,
~JESUS, HELP ME.
In disappointments, troubles, and sorrows,
~JESUS, HELP ME.
When I throw myself on your tender love
as Father and Savior,
~JESUS, HELP ME.
When I feel impatient and my cross is heavy,
~JESUS, HELP ME.
When I am ill and my head and hands cannot do
their work,
~JESUS, HELP ME.
Always, always, in joys or sorrows, in falls
and shortcomings,
~JESUS, HELP ME.

John A. Hardon, SJ (1914–2000)[17]

Prayer Before a Crucifix

Good Jesus, friend of all,
I kneel before you hanging on the cross
and recall with sorrow and affection
your five precious wounds,
while I ponder the prophetic words
of King David your ancestor:
"They have pierced my hands and my feet.
I can count all my bones" (Psalm 22:17).
Good Jesus, crucified for me,

fix this image of yourself in my heart:
fill me with lively sentiments of faith, hope, and
    love,
make me truly sorry for my sins,
and utterly committed to your holy Gospel.
    Amen.[18]

Prayer to Our Redeemer

Soul of Christ make me holy.
Body of Christ make me whole.
Blood of Christ fill me with new life.
Water from Christ's side wash me clean.
Passion of Christ make me strong.
O good Jesus listen to me.
Within your wounds hide me.
Keep me close to you.
From the enemy defend me.
At the hour of death call me,
That with all your saints,
I may praise you, for ever. Amen.[19]

A Prayer of Self-Dedication

Lord my God,
rescue me from myself,
and give me to you.
Take away everything that draws me from you,
and give me all those things that lead me to you;
for the sake of Christ our Lord. Amen.

Abbot Louis de Blois (1506–1566) [20]

A Prayer to the Blessed Virgin Mary

We turn to you for protection,
holy Mother of God.
Listen to our prayers
and help us in our needs.
Save us from every danger,
glorious and blessed Virgin.[21]

Spiritual Communion

It is beneficial to cultivate a desire for full union
with Christ through the practice of spiritual
communion, praised by Pope John Paul II and
recommended by saints who were masters
of the spiritual life.

Pope Benedict XVI, *Sacramentum Caritatis*, # 55

Spiritual communion is a valuable practice for those
who cannot actually receive Holy Communion but
desire to do so: people in mortal sin who wish to
change their life and receive the sacrament of reconciliation; prisoners; homebound; those unable to attend
Mass on occasion; those who cannot drive to church;
those who want to receive Communion every day but
are impeded from doing so; and the very sick and the
dying who will find consolation through frequent spiritual communion.

St. Catherine of Siena on Spiritual Communion:

There are two ways in which we may
communicate—actually and spiritually. To
communicate spiritually is to do so by true and
ardent desire, and this desire ought not to exist
only at the moment of Communion, but at all
times and in all places; for it is a question of
feeding the soul with the food which sustains the
life of grace.

St. Catherine of Siena (1347–1380)[22]

An Act of Spiritual Communion by St. Alphonsus:

My Jesus, I believe that you are truly present in the Blessed Sacrament of the Altar. I love you above all things, and long for you in my soul. Since I cannot now receive you sacramentally, come at least spiritually into my heart. As though you have already come, I embrace you and unite myself entirely to you; never permit me to be separated from you.

St. Alphonsus de Liguori (1696–1787),
Doctor of the Church[23]

Prayer of the Day of the Lord:

Let us love Jesus' body in the Eucharist. Let us love the Lord's body in the bodies of the poor and of our brothers and sisters. The other's weakness is that of God's. Let us go and visit those who are alone; let us honor the Corpus Domini [Lord's Body] by stopping in front of those who ask and by making them beautiful with love. Venerating his body, broken and poured out on the altar, will make us love the weakness of God's body in the smallest of his brothers and sisters. Lord, welcome everyone in your kingdom of salvation. Remain with us, Lord. Amen.[24]

A Preparation for Holy Communion in the Home

Many people are homebound—temporarily or permanently—but a Eucharistic minister (priest, deacon, or other designated person) brings them Holy Communion so that they may share in the celebration of the Eucharistic community.

This form of prayer is meant to prepare the person to receive Communion devoutly before the Eucharistic minister arrives at the home, hospital, nursing home, hospice, or prison. It may be led by any family member or friend. In the sick person's room, it is customary to prepare a table with a crucifix, candles, and a clean white cloth for the convenience of the Eucharistic minister.

LEADER: In the name of the Father, † and of the Son, and of the Holy Spirit.

ALL: ~AMEN.

LEADER: Blessed be Jesus in the Most Holy Sacrament of the Altar.

ALL: ~BLESSED BE HIS HOLY NAME, NOW AND FOR EVER. AMEN.

The leader of prayer alternates the stanzas of the hymn with the group.

HYMN TO JESUS
O Jesus, joy of loving hearts,
The fount of life and our true light,
We seek the peace your love imparts
And stand rejoicing in your sight.

Your truth unchanged has ever stood;
You save all those who heed your call;
To those who seek you, you are good,
To those who find you, all in all.

We taste you, Lord, our living bread,
And long to feast upon you still;
We drink of you, the fountainhead,
Our thirsting souls to quench and fill.

For you are restless spirit yearns,
Where'er our changing lot is cast;
Glad, when your presence we discern,
Blest when our faith can hold you fast.

O Jesus, with us ever stay;
Make all our moments calm and bright;
Oh, chase the night of sin away,
Shed o'er the world your holy light.

St. Bernard of Clairvaux (1091–1153)[25]

A UNIVERSAL HYMN OF PRAISE

PSALM 117   NAB

The leader of prayer begins the antiphon to the
asterisk *, and recites the verses of the psalm while
the group repeats the antiphon.

ANTIPHON Christ is victor,* CHRIST IS RULER,
    CHRIST IS LORD OF ALL!

Praise the LORD, all you nations!
    Give glory, all you peoples!
~CHRIST IS VICTOR, CHRIST IS RULER, CHRIST IS
    LORD OF ALL!

A Preparation for Holy Communion in the Home **19**

The LORD's love for us is strong;
   The LORD is faithful for ever.
~CHRIST IS VICTOR, CHRIST IS RULER, CHRIST IS
   LORD OF ALL!

Glory to the Father, and to the Son,
   and to the Holy Spirit:
~CHRIST IS VICTOR, CHRIST IS RULER, CHRIST IS
   LORD OF ALL!

As it was in the beginning, is now,
   and will be for ever. Amen.
~CHRIST IS VICTOR, CHRIST IS RULER, CHRIST IS
   LORD OF ALL!

PSALM PRAYER

LEADER: Let us pray (pause for silent prayer):

Holy, mighty, and immortal God,
glorified by the cherubim,
worshipped by the seraphim,
and adored by all the powers of heaven:
You created us in your own image
and restored and adorned us with every good gift
in Jesus-Messiah, our Lord and Savior.
Be pleased to accept our hymns of praise,
sanctify our souls and bodies,
and forgive us our transgressions;
for you are holy, O God, and we glorify you,
Father, Son, and Holy Spirit,
now and always, and for ever and ever.
ALL: ~AMEN.

A Reading from the Holy Gospel According to St. John 6:53–58

READER: So Jesus said to them, "Very truly, I tell you, unless you eat the flesh of the Son of Man and drink his blood, you have no life in you. Those who eat my flesh and drink my blood have eternal life, and I will raise them up on the last day; for my flesh is true food and my blood is true drink. Those who eat my flesh and drink my blood abide in me, and I in them. Just as the living Father sent me, and I live because of the Father, so whoever eats me will live because of me. This is the bread that came down from heaven, not like that which your ancestors ate, and they died. But the one who eats this bread will live for ever."

ALL: ~PRAISE TO YOU, LORD JESUS CHRIST.

Pause for Quiet Prayer

RESPONSE
LEADER: My flesh is true food, alleluia!
ALL: ~AND MY BLOOD IS TRUE DRINK, ALLELUIA!

A LITANY OF THE BLESSED SACRAMENT
(see pages 40-42)

THE LORD'S PRAYER
LEADER: Let us pray as Jesus taught us:
    Our Father in heaven,
    HALLOWED BE YOUR NAME,
    YOUR KINGDOM COME,

YOUR WILL BE DONE,
ON EARTH AS IN HEAVEN.
GIVE US TODAY OUR DAILY BREAD.
FORGIVE US OUR SINS
AS WE FORGIVE THOSE WHO SIN AGAINST US.
SAVE US FROM THE TIME OF TRIAL
AND DELIVER US FROM EVIL.
FOR THE KINGDOM, THE POWER, AND THE
GLORY ARE YOURS NOW AND FOR EVER.
AMEN.

CLOSING PRAYER

LEADER: Lord Jesus Christ,
you gave us the Eucharist
as the memorial of your suffering and death.
May our worship of this sacrament
of your body and blood
help us to experience the salvation
you won for us
and the peace of the kingdom
where you live with the Father and the Holy Spirit,
one God, for ever and ever.
ALL: ~AMEN.[26]

Blessed be Jesus in the Most Holy Sacrament of
the Altar.
ALL: ~AMEN.

See also the many Eucharistic prayers on pages 2-12,
which will be helpful for the sick and dying and those
about to receive Viaticum (food for the journey—the
journey of death).

Part 2
Adoration of the Blessed Sacrament

The Eucharist is not only a festal meal but an abiding and personal Presence of Jesus, body and blood, soul and divinity, in the tabernacle. No distant God is he! Whatever our needs, Jesus is there for our worship and our consolation.

> "Amen. Come, Lord Jesus!"
> **Revelation 22:20**

To *adore* the Blessed Sacrament means to worship, hallow, honor, respect, reverence, venerate, and pray to the living Lord Jesus reserved in the Blessed Sacrament of the Altar. To *adore* also means to be devout, consecrated, serious, and zealous in regard to the Blessed Sacrament in both a very inner and practical way. It means to be as prepared as possible to acknowledge the divine and human Presence of our Savior in the tabernacle and to be as present to him as our human powers permit. We are not as strong as he is but we can learn how, by his grace, to rally our forces of mind and spirit and so enjoy our precious minutes and hours before the Blessed Sacrament. It is an enormous privilege to be an adorer of Jesus, the light and the life of the world!

Since a portion of the Holy Eucharist is reserved after Mass for the sake of the sick and dying, over the centuries believers have become more and more aware of the sacramental Presence in our churches. Our consciousness of Jesus present in our tabernacles shows itself by external signs of our devout belief: a reverent silence in church at all times, genuflections before entering our pews, bows before receiving Holy Communion, reception of both the consecrated bread and wine, a time of thanksgiving after Communion, and special reverence and personal attention, at all times, toward the Blessed Sacrament itself.

Several private and public forms of devotion have also grown up to satisfy and encourage such devotion; for example, visits of prayer before the reserved Sacrament in the tabernacle, benediction of the Blessed Sacrament, holy hours of prayer before the tabernacle or before the Host exposed in a monstrance, perpetual adoration, nocturnal adoration, the Forty Hours devotion, and processions with the Blessed Sacrament on Holy Thursday, Corpus Christi, and other special occasions.

Perpetual adoration and nocturnal adoration of the Blessed Sacrament became widely popular in the nineteenth century. It was often a kind of spiritual reparation for all the damages caused to the church by revolutionary and secular Europe. It was also a form of reparation for sacrileges committed against the Blessed Sacrament and for the coldness and irreverence of lukewarm Catholics who had little or no devotion to the Divine Sacrament in our tabernacles. In addition, it became a spontaneous and effective way of proclaiming the Catholic faith and of expressing the growing piety of those who truly love the sacramental system.

In our time, perpetual—that is, continuous—adoration of the Blessed Sacrament is growing in popularity. Parishes with adoration chapels are becoming more and more common and are bringing about a deeper devotion to the Blessed Sacrament. They try to maintain perpetual adoration of the reserved Sacrament by relays of two or more people by day and by night. The team, with vocal prayer and silent adoration, passes an hour of adoration fruitfully for themselves, for their parish, and for the worldwide church. As a result such parishes find that they experience a significant spiritual and parochial revival.

Many parishes often observe nocturnal adoration at least once a week or month—usually from Thursday evening to Friday morning and often on the First Friday of the month.

Words of Adoration

Pope John Paul II Speaks:

The mystery of the Eucharist—sacrifice, presence, banquet—*does not allow for reduction or exploitation;* it must be experienced and lived in its integrity, both in its celebration and in the intimate converse with Jesus which takes place after receiving communion or in a prayerful moment of Eucharistic adoration apart from Mass. These are the times when the Church is firmly built up and it becomes clear what she truly is: one, holy, catholic, and apostolic; the people, temple, and family of God; the body and the bride of Christ, enlivened by the Holy Spirit; the universal sacrament of salvation and a hierarchically structured communion.

Pope John Paul II (1920–2005)[27]

Hear the Words of St. Francis of Assisi:

The whole world should tremble and heavens
      rejoice,
when Christ, the Son of the living God,
is present on the altar in the hands of the priest.
What wonderful majesty! What stupendous
      condescension!
O sublime humility! O humble sublimity!
That the Lord of the whole universe, God and the
      Son of God,
should humble himself like this

and hide under the form of a little bread for our
      salvation.
Look at God's condescension, my brothers,
and *pour out your hearts before him* (Psalm 61:9).
Humble yourselves that you may be exalted by
      him (cf. 1 Peter 5:6).
Keep nothing for yourselves
so that he who has given himself wholly to you
may receive you wholly.

St. Francis of Assisi (1181–1226)[28]

Hear the Words of St. Alphonsus de Liguori:

Many Christians make great efforts and put
themselves in great danger to visit the sites of the
Holy Land, where our most loving Savior was
born, suffered, and died. We do not need to make
such a long voyage or face so many dangers. The
same Lord is near us and lives in the church but a
few steps away from our homes. Pilgrims consider
it a great fortune, says St. Paulinus, to bring back
a bit of dust from holy sites such as the nativity
shrine or the sepulcher where Jesus was buried.
Shouldn't we visit the Most Holy Sacrament where
the same Jesus is in person, and where we can
safely go with little effort with even ardor?"

St. Alphonsus de Liguori (1696–1787),
Doctor of the Church[29]

Hear the Words of Thomas Merton:

In order to sink our roots deeper into the charity of Christ, it is necessary that we seek opportunities to adore Christ in the Blessed Sacrament and to give testimony to our faith outside the time of Mass. Therefore we visit our churches in order to pray to him in silence and alone. We go to benediction of the Blessed Sacrament. We make Holy Hours, or we spend time in adoration, by day and by night, before the sacramental Christ enthroned upon the altar. All these contacts deepen our awareness of the great mystery that is the very heart of the Church and open our souls to the influence of the Son of God "who gives life to whom he wills" (John 5:21).

Thomas Merton (1915–1968)[30]

Hear the Words of Pope John Paul II:

The Magisterium's commitment to proclaiming the Eucharistic Mystery has been matched by the interior growth within the Christian community. Certainly the liturgical reform inaugurated by the [Second Vatican] Council has greatly contributed to a more conscious, active, and fruitful participation in the Holy Sacrifice of the Altar on the part of the faithful. In many places, adoration of the Blessed Sacrament is also an important daily practice and has become an inexhaustible source of holiness. The devout participation of the faithful in the Eucharistic procession of the Solemnity of the Body and Blood of Christ is a grace from the Lord which yearly brings joy to those who take part in it.

Pope John Paul II (1920–2005)[31]

Hear the Words of Pope Benedict XVI:

I heartily recommend to the Church's pastors and to the People of God, the practice of Eucharistic adoration, both individually and in community. Great benefit would ensue from a suitable catechesis explaining this act of worship, which enables the faithful to experience the liturgical celebration more fully and more fruitfully. Wherever possible it would be appropriate, especially in densely populated areas, to set aside specific churches or oratories for perpetual adoration. I would also like to encourage those associations of the faithful and confraternities specifically devoted to eucharistic adoration; they serve as a leaven of contemplation for the whole Church and a summons to individuals and communities to place Christ at the center of their lives.

Pope Benedict XVI (1927–)[32]

Brief Devotions to the Blessed Sacrament

These brief devotions will help those who want to initiate themselves by using relatively short prayers before the tabernacle before going on to longer visits to the Blessed Sacrament later in this book.

Antiphon

How sacred is the feast *
IN WHICH YOU ARE OUR FOOD,
THE MEMORIAL OF YOUR SUFFERINGS
    IS CELEBRATED ANEW,
OUR HEARTS ARE FILLED WITH GRACE,
AND WE ARE GIVEN A PLEDGE
OF THE GLORY THAT IS TO COME, ALLELUIA!

You give us manna from heaven, alleluia!
~SENDING DOWN BREAD FOR US TO EAT,
    ALLELUIA!

Let us pray for true devotion to the Blessed
    Sacrament:

Lord Jesus Christ,
high priest of the new and eternal covenant,
you feed our souls and bodies
with your sacramental body and blood,
and abide on our altars as our source
of ever-ready comfort and consolation.
Remind us each day that you are truly with us,

have us rejoice in your loving presence,
and steer us toward the doors of heaven,
where you live and reign for ever and ever.
~AMEN.[33]

A Prayer in Full Faith

Give me, good Lord, a full faith and a fervent
    charity,
a love of you, good Lord,
incomparable above the love of myself;
and that I love nothing to your displeasure
but everything in an order to you.

Take from me, good Lord, this lukewarm fashion,
or rather this cold manner of meditation
and this dullness in praying to you.
And give me warmth, delight, and life
in thinking about you.
And give me your grace to long for your holy
    sacraments
and specially to rejoice in the presence of your
    blessed body and blood,
sweet Savior, in the holy sacrament of the altar,
and duly to thank you for your gracious coming.
    Amen.

St. Thomas More (1478–1535), English martyr[34]

A Prayer Before the Blessed Sacrament

O Jesus, present in the sacrament of the altar,
teach all nations to serve you with a willing heart,
knowing that to serve God is to reign.

May your sacrament, O Jesus,
be light to the mind,
strength to the will,
joy to the heart.
May it be the support of the weak,
the comfort of the suffering,
the wayfaring bread of salvation for the dying,
and, for all, the pledge of future glory. Amen.

Blessed Pope John XXIII (1881–1963)[35]

A Short Visit to the Blessed Sacrament

I place myself in the presence of Him,
in whose Incarnate Presence I am before
I place myself there.

I adore you, O my Savior,
present here as God and Man,
in soul and body,
in true flesh and blood.

I acknowledge and confess
that I kneel before that Sacred Humanity,
which was conceived in Mary's womb,
and lay on Mary's bosom;
which grew up to man's estate,
and by the Sea of Galilee called the Twelve,
wrought miracles,
and spoke words of wisdom and peace;
which in due season hung on the cross,
lay in the tomb, rose from the dead,
and now reigns in heaven.

I praise, and bless, and give myself wholly to Him,
who is the true Bread of my soul,
and my everlasting joy.

John Henry Cardinal Newman (1801–1890)[36]

Jesus, My Friend

Lord Jesus, friend of the human race,
and my personal friend too:
You are close to me at every moment of my day,
You are teaching me how to live,
You show me how to be a friend to others,
You are helping me prepare for eternity.
You passed through the dark valley of death
but rose on Easter morning,
the light and life of the world.
Draw me to your Sacred Heart
in the Blessed Sacrament of the Altar
and make me your personal disciple,
a friend of your Mother and of all the saints in
        glory.
Glory to God, alleluia! Glory to God! Amen.

Hail, Sacred Heart of Jesus

Hail, Heart of my Jesus: save me!
Hail, Heart of my Creator: perfect me!
Hail, Heart of my Savior: deliver me!
Hail, Heart of my Judge: pardon me!
Hail, Heart of my Father: govern me!
Hail, Heart of my Master: teach me!

Hail, Heart of my King: crown me!
Hail, Heart of my Benefactor: enrich me!
Hail, Heart of my Pastor: guard me!
Hail Heart of my Brother: stay with me!
Hail, Heart of my Incomparable Goodness:
     have mercy on me.
Hail, most Loving Heart: inflame me! Amen.

St. Margaret Mary Alacoque (1647–1690)

To the Sacred Heart of Jesus

O my God!
I offer you all my actions of this day
for the intentions and the glory of the Sacred
     Heart of Jesus.
I desire to sanctify every beat of my heart,
by uniting them to its infinite merits,
and I wish to make reparation for my sins
by casting them into the furnace of its merciful
     love.
O my God!
I ask you for myself and for those I hold dear
the grace to fulfill your holy will perfectly,
to accept for love of you
the joys and sorrows of this passing life,
so that we may one day be united in heaven
for all eternity. Amen.

St. Thérèse of Lisieux (1873–1897)

Seven Visits to the
Blessed Sacrament

> I encourage all Christians to make regular visits
> to Christ in the Blessed Sacrament of the Altar.
> We are all called to remain permanently in the
> presence of God, thanks to Him who remains
> with us to the end of the age.
>
> Pope John Paul II (1920–2005)[37]

The following seven days of prayer—combining hymns,
psalms, prayers, readings from the Bible and the Holy
Fathers, and intercessions—are designed to help us
pause in prayer and contemplation before the Blessed
Sacrament whenever we can. They may be used by
groups of people who would like to spend time together
before the tabernacle, but they are also designed for
the personal and private prayer of individuals. This
combination of Word and Sacrament is another devout
way of assimilating the Holy Gospel by listening to our
Lord's actual words recorded in the Holy Gospels in
the very presence of his divine person in the Blessed
Sacrament.

The pauses indicated for silent adoration should last
for several minutes.

Day One

We make the sign of the cross with the first versicle.

LEADER: Blessed ✝ be Jesus in the Most Holy
Sacrament of the Altar!

ALL: ~AMEN. ALLELUIA!

The leader alternates the stanzas of the hymn with
the group.

HYMN

Hail our Savior's glorious Body,
Which his Virgin Mother bore;
Hail the Blood, which shed for sinners,
Did a broken world restore.
Hail the sacrament most holy,
Flesh and Blood of Christ adore!

To the Virgin, for our healing,
His own Son the Father sends;
From the Father's love proceeding
Sower, seed, and Word descends;
Wondrous life of Word incarnate
With his greatest wonder ends!

On that paschal evening see him
With the chosen twelve recline,
To the old law still obedient
In its feast of love divine;
Love divine the new law giving,
Gives himself as Bread and Wine!

Glory be to God the Father,
Praise to his co-equal Son,
Adoration to the Spirit,
Bond of love, in Godhead one!
Blest be God by all creation
Joyously while ages run!

St. Thomas Aquinas, (1225–1274)[38]

The leader begins the antiphon to the asterisk * and
alternates the stanzas of the psalm with the group.

PSALM 42:2–6   LONGING FOR GOD'S PRESENCE NAB

ANTIPHON I will come to the altar of God, *
TO GOD, MY JOY, MY DELIGHT.

As the deer longs for streams of water,
    so my soul longs for you, O God.
My being thirsts for God, the living God.
    When can I go and see the face of God?
My tears have been my food day and night,
    as they ask daily, "Where is your God?"

Those times I recall
    as I pour out my soul.
When I went in procession with the crowd,
    I went with them to the house of God,
Amid loud cries of thanksgiving,
    with the multitude keeping festival.

Why are you cast down, my soul;
    why do you groan within me?
Wait for God, whom I shall praise again,
    my Savior and my God.

All repeat the antiphon in unison.

ANTIPHON I WILL COME TO THE ALTAR OF GOD, TO GOD, MY JOY, MY DELIGHT.

PSALM PRAYER

Let us pray (pause for quiet adoration):

LEADER: Our Father, our God,
we remember all you have done for us
because of the great memorial
created by your dear Son, our Savior,
on the night before he died for us.
Give us the grace to praise and adore
   his holy presence
in the Blessed Sacrament of the Altar,
now and always and for ever and ever.
ALL: ~AMEN.

A reader takes both readings.

FIRST READING **THE LAST SUPPER** **1 CORINTHIANS 11:23–26**

READER: For I received from the Lord what I also handed on to you, that the Lord Jesus on the night when he was betrayed took a loaf of bread, and when he had given thanks, he broke it and said, "This is my body that is broken for you. Do this in remembrance of me." In the same way he took the cup also, after supper, saying, "This cup is the new covenant in my blood. Do this, as often as you drink it, in remembrance of me."

Pause for Silent Adoration

RESPONSORY

LEADER: As often as you eat this bread and drink this cup,

ALL: ~As often as you eat this bread and drink this cup,

LEADER: You proclaim the Lord's death until he comes,

ALL: ~As often as you eat this bread and drink this cup,

LEADER: Glory to the Father, and to the Son, and to the Holy Spirit,

ALL: ~As often as you eat this bread and drink this cup.

SECOND READING   JUDGE BY FAITH

READER: This teaching of blessed Paul is in itself sufficient to assure you fully on the divine mysteries. . . . Since then Christ himself clearly described the bread to us in the words, "This is my body," who will dare dispute it? And since he has emphatically said, "This is my blood," who will waver in the slightest and say it is not his blood?

By his own power on a previous occasion he turned water into wine at Cana of Galilee; so it is surely credible that he has changed wine into his blood. If he performed that wonderful miracle just because he had been invited to a human marriage, we shall certainly be much more willing to admit that he has conferred on the wedding guests the savoring of his body and blood. . . .

Do not, then, regard the bread and wine as nothing but bread and wine, for they are the body and blood of Christ, as the Master himself has proclaimed. Though your senses suggest to you, let faith reassure you. Do not judge the matter by taste but by faith, which brings you certainty without doubting, since you have been found worthy of Christ's body and blood.

St. Cyril of Jerusalem (ca. 315–386)[39]

Pause for Silent Adoration

RESPONSORY
LEADER: Examine yourself, and only then
ALL: ~EAT OF THE BREAD AND DRINK OF THE CUP.

A LITANY OF THE BLESSED SACRAMENT

Lord, have mercy.	~LORD, HAVE MERCY.
Christ, have mercy.	~CHRIST, HAVE MERCY.
Lord, have mercy.	~LORD, HAVE MERCY.
God our Father in heaven,	~HAVE MERCY ON US.
God the Son, Redeemer of the world,	~HAVE MERCY ON US.
God the Holy Spirit,	~HAVE MERCY ON US.
Holy Trinity, one God,	~HAVE MERCY ON US.
Word made flesh and living among us,	~HAVE MERCY ON US.
Pure and acceptable sacrifice,	~HAVE MERCY ON US.
Hidden manna from above,	~HAVE MERCY ON US.

Living bread that came down
from heaven,   ~HAVE MERCY ON US.
Bread of life for a hungry world,   ~HAVE MERCY ON US.
Chalice of blessing,   ~HAVE MERCY ON US.
Precious blood that washes
away our sins,   ~HAVE MERCY ON US.
Memorial of God's undying love, ~HAVE MERCY ON US.
Food that lasts for eternal life,   ~HAVE MERCY ON US.
Mystery of faith,   ~HAVE MERCY ON US.
Medicine of immortality,   ~HAVE MERCY ON US.
Food of God's chosen,   ~HAVE MERCY ON US.
Perpetual presence in our
tabernacles,   ~HAVE MERCY ON US.
Viaticum of those who die in
the Lord,   ~HAVE MERCY ON US.
Pledge of future glory,   ~HAVE MERCY ON US.

By the great longing you
had to eat the Passover
with your disciples   ~GOOD LORD, DELIVER US.
By your humble example
of washing their feet,   ~GOOD LORD, DELIVER US.
By your loving gift of this
divine sacrament,   ~GOOD LORD, DELIVER US.
By your five precious wounds,   ~GOOD LORD, DELIVER US.
By your sacrificial death
on the cross,   ~GOOD LORD, DELIVER US.
By the piercing of your
sacred heart,   ~GOOD LORD, DELIVER US.
By the outpouring of blood
and water,   ~GOOD LORD, DELIVER US.
By your victorious rising
on the third day,   ~GOOD LORD, DELIVER US.
By your wondrous ascension
into heaven,   ~GOOD LORD, DELIVER US.

By your gift of the Paraclete
Spirit, ~GOOD LORD, DELIVER US.

By your return in glory to
judge the living and
the dead, ~GOOD LORD, DELIVER US.

Lamb of God, you take away the
sins of the world, ~HAVE MERCY ON US.

Lamb of God, you take away the
sins of the world, ~HAVE MERCY ON US.

Lamb of God, you take away the sins of the world,
~GRANT US YOUR PEACE.

LEADER: You gave them bread from heaven to be
their food.

ALL: ~AND THIS BREAD CONTAINED ALL
GOODNESS.

CLOSING PRAYER

LEADER: Lord Jesus Christ,
you gave us the Eucharist
as the memorial of your suffering and death.
May our worship of this sacrament
of your body and blood
help us to experience the salvation you won for us
and the peace of your kingdom,
where you live with the Father and the Holy Spirit,
one God, for ever and ever.

ALL: ~AMEN.[40]

DOXOLOGY

LEADER: May the heart of Jesus in the Most Blessed
Sacrament

be praised, adored, and loved, with grateful
affection,

at every moment, in all the tabernacles of the
world,

even to the end of time.

ALL: ~AMEN.

With groups of adorers, the directions (rubrics)
printed in Day One are used each day.

Day Two

Blessed ✝ be Jesus in the Most Holy Sacrament
of the altar!

~AMEN. ALLELUIA!

HYMN

By his word the Word almighty
Makes of bread his flesh indeed;
Wine becomes his very life-blood;
Faith God's living Word must heed!
Faith alone may safely guide us
Where the senses cannot lead.

Come, adore his wondrous presence;
Bow to Christ, the source of grace!
Here is kept the sacred promise
Of God's earthly dwelling-place!
Sight is blind before God's glory,
Faith alone may see his face!

Glory be to God the Father,
Praise to his co-equal Son,
Adoration to the Spirit,
Bond of love, in Godhead one!
Blest be God by all creation
Joyously while ages run!

St. Thomas Aquinas (1225–1274)[41]

ANTIPHON My flesh is true food * AND MY BLOOD
IS TRUE DRINK.

O my people, hear my teaching;
    incline your ears to the words of my mouth.
I will open my mouth in a parable;
    I will utter dark sayings from of old,
things that we have heard and known,
    that our ancestors have told us.

We will not hide them from their children,
    but tell to the coming generation
the glorious deeds of the Lord, the might
    and wonders God has wrought.

The Lord commanded the skies above,
    opened the doors of heaven,
rained down on them manna to eat,
    and gave them the grain of heaven.

Mortals ate the bread of angels;
    God sent them food in abundance,
caused the east wind to blow in the heavens,
    and let out the south wind in power.

God rained flesh down upon them like dust,
    winged birds like the sand of the seas;
God let them fall within their camp,
    all around their dwellings.

ANTIPHON MY FLESH IS TRUE FOOD AND MY BLOOD
IS TRUE DRINK.

Psalm Prayer

Let us pray (pause for quiet adoration):

God of our ancestors in the faith,
you provide for us in all our needs.
Remember the deeds you did of old
for the people who put their trust in you
and give the people of the new covenant
the precious body and blood of your dear Son
as food for our journey toward Paradise.
Blest be the holy name of Jesus!
~Amen.

First Reading	Manna from Heaven	Deuteronomy 8:2–3

Remember the long way that the Lord your God has led you these forty years in the wilderness, in order to humble you, testing you to know what was in your heart, whether or not you would keep his commandments. He humbled you by letting you hunger, then feeding you with manna, with which neither you nor your ancestors were acquainted, in order to make you understand that one does not live by bread alone, but by every word that comes from the mouth of the Lord.

Pause for Silent Adoration

Responsory

God rained down manna for their food,
~And gave them bread from heaven.

Who is the author of the sacraments except the
Lord Jesus? These sacraments came from heaven,
for all God's purpose is from heaven. Still, it
remains true that that when God rained down
manna for the people from heaven, and the people
ate without working for their food, this was a
great and divine sign.

Perhaps you say, "The bread I have here is
ordinary bread." Yes, before the sacramental words
are uttered this bread is nothing but bread. But at the
consecration the bread becomes the body of Christ.
Let us reason this out. How can something that is
bread be the body of Christ? Well, by what words
is the consecration effected, and whose words are
they? The words of the Lord Jesus. All that is said
before are the words of the priest: praise is offered
to God, the prayer is offered up, petitions are made
for the people, for kings, for all others. But when the
moment comes for bringing the most holy sacrament
into being, the priest does not use his own words any
longer: he uses the words of Christ. Therefore, it is
Christ's word that brings the sacrament into being.

St. Ambrose of Milan (ca. 339–397)[42]

Pause for Silent Adoration

RESPONSORY
Jesus said to them, "I am the living bread
~THAT CAME DOWN FROM HEAVEN."

A Litany of the Blessed Sacrament
(see pages 40–42)

CLOSING PRAYER
Gracious Father,
your loving providence
is our strength and our delight.
We thank you from the bottom of our heart
for your great and precious gift of Christ's
abiding presence on our altars.
We believe that Jesus is here for us,
body and blood, soul and divinity.
in the fullness of his divine personhood.
As you fed your ancient people of Israel,
feed us now with the true bread
that comes down from heaven
and gives life to the world.
Your kingdom come!
~Amen.

DOXOLOGY
May the heart of Jesus in the Most Blessed
        Sacrament
be praised, adored, and loved, with grateful
        affection,
at every moment, in all the tabernacles of the
        world,
even to the end of time.
~Amen.

Day Three

Blessed ✝ be Jesus in the Most Holy Sacrament
   of the altar!

~AMEN. ALLELUIA!

HYMN

From on high the Father sends
His Son, who yet stays by his side.
The Word made for us then spends
His life till life's last eventide.

While Judas plans the traitor's sign,
The mocking kiss that Love betrays,
Jesus in form of bread and wine
His loving sacrifice displays.

He gives himself that faith may see
The heavenly food on which we feed,
That flesh and blood in us may be
Fed by his Flesh and Blood indeed.

O Priest and Victim, Lord of Life,
Throw wide the gates of Paradise!
We face our foes in mortal strife;
You are our strength! O heed our cries!

St. Thomas Aquinas (1225–1274)[43]

PSALM 23   SHEPHERD AND HOST

ANTIPHON You prepare a table before me, *
MY CUP OVERFLOWS.

The Lord is my shepherd, I shall not want;
    the Lord makes me lie down in green
    pastures,   .
leads me beside still waters;
    restores my life,
leads me in right paths
    for the sake of the Lord's name.

Even though I walk through the darkest valley,
    I fear no evil;
for you are with me;
    your rod and your staff,
    they comfort me.

You prepare a table before me
    in the presence of my enemies;
you anoint my head with oil,
    my cup overflows.

Only goodness and mercy shall follow me
    all the days of my life;
and I shall dwell in the house of the Lord
    as long as I live.

ANTIPHON YOU PREPARE A TABLE BEFORE ME,
MY CUP OVERFLOWS.

PSALM PRAYER
Let us pray (pause for quiet adoration):

Good shepherd of the flock,
guide us along the right path
and deliver us from all our fears.

Your sacramental presence among us
assures us you are always with us.
You anoint us with the oil of salvation,
feed us with the finest wheat,
and make us sit at your welcome table,
now and for ever.
~Amen.

First Reading The Pure Offering   Malachi 1:11
From the rising of the sun to its setting my
name is great among the nations, and in every
place incense is offered to my name, and a pure
offering; for my name is great among the nations,
says the Lord of hosts.

Pause for Silent Adoration

Responsory
The Lord is my light and my salvation.
~Whom shall I fear?

Second Reading   The Sacrament of the Altar
No other sacrament can be more wholesome. By
it sins are purged away; virtues are increased; and
the soul is enriched with an abundance of every
spiritual gift. The church offers it for both the
living and the dead so that what was instituted for
all might be to the advantage of all. We cannot
fully express the attractiveness of this sacrament
in which we taste spiritual delight at its source
and in which we renew the surpassing love which

Christ revealed to us in his passion. In order to impress the immensity of his love for us, at the last supper, while celebrating the Passover Meal with his disciples, he instituted this sacrament as a perpetual memorial of his passion, as the fulfillment of all the Old Testament types, as the greatest of his miracles, and as a unique consolation for his physical absence.

St. Thomas Aquinas (1225–1274)[44]

Pause for Silent Adoration

RESPONSORY

As often as you eat this bread and drink this cup,
~YOU SHOW FORTH THE DEATH OF THE LORD
UNTIL HE COMES.

A LITANY OF THE BLESSED SACRAMENT
(see pages 40–42)

CLOSING PRAYER

Lord and Savior of the world,
by the reception of Holy Communion,
you nourish us with your life-giving body and
blood
that unites your holy Church in heaven and on
earth.
Make us ever faithful to the vows of our Baptism
and inspire us to celebrate the Holy Eucharist
with increasing faith and fervor

as we pray for the needs of the whole world.
May the tabernacle of your presence
be the ark of the covenant for us
as we adore you unceasingly,
in union with all the saints
who long for the coming of your kingdom.
You live and reign, now and for ever.
~Amen.

Doxology
May the heart of Jesus in the Most Blessed
Sacrament
be praised, adored, and loved, with grateful
affection,
at every moment, in all the tabernacles of the
world,
even to the end of time.
~Amen.

Day Four

Blessed † be Jesus in the Most Holy Sacrament
   of the altar!
~AMEN. ALLELUIA!

HYMN

At this great feast of love
Let joyful praise resound,
Let heartfelt knowledge now ascend
To heaven's height:
Ring out the reign of sin;
Ring in the reign of grace;
A world renewed acclaims its King,
Though veiled from sight.

Recall the night when Christ
Proclaims his law of love,
And shows himself as Lamb of God
And great high priest:
The sinless One, made sin,
For sinners gives his all,
And shares with us his very self
As Paschal feast.

The bread that angels eat
Becomes our food on earth,
God sends his manna, living Bread,
From heaven above:
What wonders now we see:
Those who are last and least

Receive their Lord as food and drink,
His pledge of love.

Three persons, yet one God,
Be pleased to hear our prayer:
Come down in power to seek your own,
dispel our night;
Teach us your word of truth;
Guide us along your way;
Bring us at last to dwell with you
In endless light.

St. Thomas Aquinas (1225–1274)[45]

PSALM 43   JUDICA ME   NAB

ANTIPHON I will come to your altar, O God, *
TO GOD, MY JOY, MY DELIGHT.

Grant me justice, God;
    defend me from a faithless people;
    from the deceitful and unjust rescue me.

You, God, are my strength.
    Why then do you spurn me?
Why must I go about mourning,
    with the enemy oppressing me?

Send your light and fidelity,
    that they may be my guide
and bring me to your holy mountain,
    to the place of your dwelling,

That I may come to the altar of God,
    to God, my joy, my delight.

Then I will praise you with the harp,
O God, my God.

ANTIPHON I WILL COME TO YOUR ALTAR, O GOD,
TO GOD, MY JOY, MY DELIGHT.

PSALM PRAYER
Let us pray (pause for quiet adoration):

God of our joy,
make us rest in the tabernacle
of your loving presence among us.
Give us the spirit of adoration,
defend us from all error,
and be our protector for ever.
We ask this through Christ our Lord.
~AMEN.

FIRST READING   THE LAST SUPPER   MARK 14:22–25
While they were eating, he took a loaf of bread,
and after blessing it he broke it and gave it to his
disciples, and said, "Take, eat; this is my body."
Then he took a cup, and after giving thanks he
gave it to them, and all of them drank from it. He
said to them, "This is my blood of the covenant,
which is poured out for many for the forgiveness
of sins. Truly I tell you, I will never again drink of
the vine until that day when I drink it new in the
kingdom of God."

Pause for Silent Adoration

RESPONSORY

Jesus said to his disciples,

~"DO THIS IN REMEMBRANCE OF ME."

SECOND READING   **THE REAL PRESENCE**

You have now been taught and fully instructed
that what seems to be bread is not bread, though
it appears to be such to the sense of taste, but
the body of Christ; that what seems to be wine is
not wine, though the taste would have it so, but
the blood of Christ; that David was speaking of
this long ago when he sang, *Bread strengthens
the heart of man, that he may make his face glad
with oil* (Psalm 104:15). May you unveil it with
conscience undefiled and reflect the glory of the
Lord, and pass *from glory to glory* in Christ Jesus
our Lord. To him be honor, power, and glory for
ever and ever. Amen.

St. Cyril of Jerusalem (ca. 313–386)[46]

Pause for Silent Adoration

RESPONSORY

God opened the gates of heaven;

~MERE MORTALS ATE THE BREAD OF ANGELS.

A LITANY OF THE BLESSED SACRAMENT
(see pages 40–42)

Closing Prayer

Lord Jesus, Redeemer of the world,
you were eager to eat the Passover
with your friends on the night before you died.
Send forth your light and your truth
and lead us to the place where you dwell
in the blessed Sacrament of the Altar.
By the power of your abiding presence,
make us love you with our whole heart
and love and serve our neighbor as ourself.
You live and reign with the Father,
in the unity of the Holy Spirit,
one God, for ever and ever.
~Amen.

Doxology

May the heart of Jesus in the Most Blessed
	Sacrament
be praised, adored, and loved, with grateful
	affection,
at every moment, in all the tabernacles of the
	world,
even to the end of time
~Amen.

Day Five

Blessed ✝ be Jesus in the Most Holy Sacrament
   of the altar!

~AMEN! ALLELUIA!

HYMN

Where true love is dwelling, God is dwelling there;
love's own loving Presence love does ever share.

Love of Christ has made us out of many one;
in our midst is dwelling God's eternal Son.

Give him joyful welcome, love him and revere;
cherish one another with a love sincere.

As in Christ we gather discord has no part;
ours is but one spirit, but one mind and heart.

Bitterness now ended, let there be accord;
always with us dwelling be our God and Lord.

May we share the vision with the saints on high;
of Christ's matchless glory when we come to die.

Joy of all the blessed, be our heavenly prize;
dwell with us for ever, Lord of Paradise!

Where true love is dwelling, God is dwelling there;
love's own loving Presence love does ever share.[47]

PSALM 63:1–8   LONGING FOR GOD   NAB

ANTIPHON The words that I have spoken to you *
ARE SPIRIT AND LIFE.

O God, you are my God—
   for you I long!

For you my body yearns;
	for you my soul thirsts,
Like a land parched, lifeless,
	and without water.

So I look to you in the sanctuary
	to see your power and glory.
For your love is better than life;
	my lips offer you worship.

I will bless you as long as I live;
	I will lift up my hands, calling
	on your name,
my soul shall savor the rich banquet of praise,
	with joyous lips my mouth shall honor you!

When I think of you upon my bed,
	through the night watches I will recall
that you indeed are my help,
	and in the shadow of your wings
	I shout for joy.
My soul clings fast to you;
	your right hand upholds me.

ANTIPHON THE WORDS THAT I HAVE SPOKEN TO
	YOU ARE SPIRIT AND LIFE.

PSALM PRAYER

Let us pray (pause for quiet adoration):

Lord God, giver of peace and rest,
you reward those who thirst for you

and look to you in your tabernacle,
where mercy and faithfulness meet
and justice and peace embrace.
Blest be Christ Jesus our Lord!
~AMEN.

FIRST READING　　**BREAD FROM HEAVEN**　　**JOHN 6:27–34**

"Do not work for the food that perishes, but for the food that endures for eternal life, which the Son of Man will give you. For it is on him that God the Father has set his seal." So they said to him, "What sign are you going to give us then, so that we may see it and believe you? What work are you performing? Our ancestors ate the manna in the wilderness; as it is written, 'He gave them bread from heaven to eat.'" Then Jesus said to them, "Very truly I tell you, it was not Moses who gave you the bread from heaven, but it is my Father who gives you the true bread from heaven. For the bread of God is that which comes down from heaven and gives life to the world." They said to him, "Sir, give us this bread always."

Pause for Silent Adoration

RESPONSORY
The Lord gave them bread from heaven,
~SENDING DOWN MANNA FOR THEM TO EAT.

When you come forward [to receive Holy
Communion], do not come with arm extended or
fingers parted. Make your left hand a throne for
your right, since your right hand is to welcome
a King. Cup your palm and receive in it Christ's
Body, saying in response, *Amen*. Then carefully
bless your eyes with a touch of the holy Body, and
consume it, being careful not to drop a particle
of it, for to lose any of it is clearly like losing a
part of your own body. Tell me, if any one gave
you some gold dust, would you not keep it with
the greatest care, ensuring that that you did not
lose by dropping any of it? So you should take
still greater care not to drop a fragment of what is
more valuable than gold and precious stones.

St. Cyril of Jerusalem (ca. 313–386)[48]

Pause for Silent Adoration

RESPONSORY
We have come to believe and know
~THAT YOU ARE THE HOLY ONE OF GOD.

A LITANY OF THE BLESSED SACRAMENT
(see pages 40–42)

CLOSING PRAYER
Lord Jesus Christ,
we long and pine for your divine presence
because you have made us for yourself

and we are restless until we rest in you.
May your gracious presence on our altars
feed and calm our restless hearts
and unite us with all our fellow believers
in heaven and on earth.
Be praised and thanked,
O Savior of the world,
living and reigning with the Father,
in the unity of the Holy Spirit,
now and for ever.
~AMEN.

DOXOLOGY

May the heart of Jesus in the Most Blessed
    Sacrament
be praised, adored, and loved, with grateful
    affection,
at every moment, in all the tabernacles of the
    world,
even to the end of time.
~AMEN.

Day Six

Blessed † be Jesus in the Most Holy Sacrament
of the altar!

~AMEN. ALLELUIA!

HYMN

Zion sing in exultation,
Sing your song of jubilation,
Sing in praise of Christ your King.
Sing to Christ in adoration,
Sing the new song of salvation,
Homage to our Savior bring.

See the King his table spreading;
See the Lamb his lifeblood shedding;
See in blood the New Law sealed.
All is new, the old has vanished;
All is real, with shadows banished,
What was hidden stands revealed.

Christians, let your faith grow stronger;
What is bread is bread no longer;
Blood is here where once was wine.
Touch and sight are here deceivers,
Mind and heart, be true believers;
Truth is here beneath the sign.

Bread and wine are here concealing
What to faith God is revealing;
Outward signs his glory hide.
Bread becomes its very Giver,

Wine redemption's mighty river,
Flowing from the Savior's side.

St. Thomas Aquinas (1225–1274)[49]

PSALM 84:2–4, 9–12 THE HOUSE OF GOD   NAB

ANTIPHON Better one day in your courts *
THAN A THOUSAND ELSEWHERE!

How lovely your dwelling,
    O LORD of Hosts!
My soul yearns and pines
    for the courts of the Lord.
My heart and my flesh cry out
    for the living God.

As the sparrow finds a home
    and the swallow a nest to settle her young,
My home is by your altars,
    LORD of hosts, my King and my God!
Happy are those who dwell in your house!
    They never cease to praise you.

Better one day in your courts
    than a thousand elsewhere.
Better the threshold of the house of my God
    than a home in the tents of the wicked.
For a sun and shield is the LORD God,
    bestowing all grace and glory.

ANTIPHON BETTER ONE DAY IN YOUR COURTS
THAN A THOUSAND ELSEWHERE!

Psalm Prayer

Let us pray (pause for quiet adoration):

Lord God of all the hosts of heaven,
we long for your divine presence
in the temple of your glory.
Look on the face of your Christ
in the blessed Sacrament of the Altar
as we bow before him in adoration.
Blest be Jesus, the King of glory!
~Amen.

First Reading   The Bread of Life   John 6:45–51

Everyone who has heard and learned from the
Father comes to me. Not that any one has seen
the Father except the one who is from God; he
has seen the Father. Very truly, I tell you, whoever
believes has eternal life. I am the bread of life.
Your ancestors ate the manna in the wilderness,
and they died. This is the bread that comes down
from heaven, so that one may eat of it and not
die. I am the living bread that came down from
heaven. Whoever eats of this bread will live for
ever; and the bread that I will give for the life of
the world is my flesh.

Pause for Silent Adoration

Responsory

The bread that we break
~Is a sharing in the body of Christ.

As soon as they come up from those sacred waters [of baptism] all present embrace them, greet them, kiss them, congratulate and rejoice with them, because those who were before slaves and prisoners have all at once become free men and sons who have been invited to the royal table. For as soon as they come up from the font, they are led to the awesome table which is laden with good things. They taste the body and blood of the Lord and become the dwelling-place of the Spirit; since they have put on Christ, they go about appearing everywhere like angels on earth and shining as brightly as the rays of the sun.

St. John Chrysostom (ca. 347–407)[50]

Pause for Silent Adoration

RESPONSORY
I am with you always, alleluia!
~TO THE END OF THE AGE, ALLELUIA!

A LITANY OF THE BLESSED SACRAMENT
(see pages 40–42)

CLOSING PRAYER
Lord Jesus Christ,
as we kneel before your awesome table,
laden with the precious gifts of your body and
    blood,

may we be filled with sentiments
of praise and thanksgiving
for the endless benefits you confer on us.
Fill our hearts to overflowing with the Holy Spirit
who teaches us to pray in spirit and in truth
and to cherish our brothers and sisters
in the mystery of faith.
You live and reign with the Father,
in the unity of the Holy Spirit,
one God, for ever and ever.
~Amen.

DOXOLOGY

May the heart of Jesus in the Most Blessed
Sacrament
be praised, adored, and loved, with grateful
affection,
at every moment, in all the tabernacles of the
world,
even to the end of time.
~Amen.

Day Seven

Blessed ✝ be Jesus in the Most Holy Sacrament
   of the altar!

~AMEN, ALLELUIA!

HYMN

Christ the King, enthroned in splendor,
Comes from heaven to be our priest!
One with him as priest and victim,
One in love, we share his feast!
Praise him in high heaven above!
Praise him in this feast of love!

Light here scatters all our darkness!
Life here triumphs over death!
Come, receive from Christ in glory
God the Spirit's living breath!
Praise Christ for his victory won!
Praise the Father's firstborn Son!

Heaven is here! The gracious Father
Gives to us his only Son!
Here is sent the loving Spirit,
Making all in Christ but one!
Praise the Father, praise the Son
Praise the Spirit, Godhead one![51]

THE SUFFERING SAVIOR

CANTICLE   **1 PETER 2:21–24**

ANTIPHON We adore you, O Christ, and we bless you, * FOR BY YOUR HOLY CROSS YOU HAVE REDEEMED THE WORLD.

Christ also suffered for you,
leaving you an example,
so that you might follow
in his steps.

'He committed no sin,
and no deceit
was found in his mouth.'

When he was abused,
he did not return abuse;
when he suffered,
he did not threaten;
but entrusted himself
to the one who judges justly.

He himself bore our sins
in his body on the cross,
so that, freed from our sins,
we might live for righteousness;
by his wounds we have been healed.

ANTIPHON WE ADORE YOU, O CHRIST, AND WE BLESS YOU, FOR BY YOUR HOLY CROSS YOU HAVE REDEEMED THE WORLD.

PRAYER

Let us pray (pause for quiet adoration):

Lord Christ,
you laid down your life for us
and committed your living presence
in the blessed Sacrament of the Altar
to your Holy Catholic Church.
By your five precious wounds
in hands, feet, and side,
deliver us from our sins
and make us follow in your steps,
now and for ever.
~AMEN.

FIRST READING

TRUE FOOD AND DRINK

JOHN 6:53–58

The Lord Jesus said to them, "Very truly, I tell you, unless you eat the flesh of the Son of Man and drink his blood, you have no life in you. Those who eat my flesh and drink my blood have eternal life, and I will raise them up on the last day; for my flesh is true food and my blood is true drink. Those who eat my flesh and drink my blood abide in me and I in them. Just as the living Father sent me, and I live because of the Father, so whoever eats me will live because of me. This is the bread that comes down from heaven, not like that which your ancestors ate, and they died. But the one who eats this bread will live for ever."

Pause for Silent Adoration

RESPONSORY
By Christ's wounds
~WE HAVE BEEN HEALED.

SECOND READING   **CHRIST THE GREAT HIGH PRIEST**
The most important thing to grasp is that the food
we take is a kind of sacrifice we perform. It is true
that we commemorate our Lord's death in food
and drink, believing that these are the memorial
of his passion, since he says himself: "This is my
body which is broken for you." But it is evident
also that what we perform in the liturgy is a form
of sacrifice. The duty of the High Priest of the
New Covenant is to offer this sacrifice which
revealed the nature of the New Covenant. It is
clearly a sacrifice, although it is not something
that is new or accomplished by the efforts of the
bishop; it is a recalling of the true offering [of
Christ]. Since the bishop performs in symbol
signs of the heavenly realities, the sacrifice must
manifest them, so that he presents, as it were, an
image of the heavenly liturgy.

Theodore of Mopsuestia (ca. 350–428)[52]

Pause for Silent Adoration

RESPONSORY
The cup of blessing that we bless
~IS A SHARING IN THE BLOOD OF CHRIST.

A Litany of the Blessed Sacrament
(see pages 40–42)

Closing Prayer

Power, splendor, greatness, glory,
and honor are yours,
Lord of the Sacred Mysteries.
By sharing in the sacrifice of Golgotha
that we commemorate and celebrate
on our altars unceasingly,
may we arrive at the full expression
of our divine resemblance to you
in all the beauty of holiness.
We ask this through Christ Jesus,
our Great High Priest,
who lives and reigns with you,
in the unity of the Holy Spirit,
one God, for ever and ever.
~Amen.

Doxology

May the heart of Jesus in the Most Blessed
    Sacrament
be praised, adored, and loved, with grateful
    affection,
at every moment, in all the tabernacles of the
    world,
even to the end of time.
~Amen.

An Office of the Blessed Sacrament

A votive Office of the Blessed Sacrament often becomes a part of the schedule of prayer during adoration. Here is one example of such an office.

This office may be used by one person praying alone, by two people praying together as a team, or by a larger group of adorers with a leader. In the latter two cases, the leader officiates; alternates the versicles, hymns, psalms, and canticles with the other person or the group; supervises appropriate pauses for silent prayer of adoration; and leads the litany and the prayers. Like all such offices, we need to recite the Office of the Blessed Sacrament carefully, slowly, and with devotion. The pauses for silent prayer after the psalms and the readings should last for several minutes, and nothing should be recited in haste.

If *nocturnal* adoration begins in the evening, Evening Prayer and Night Prayer may be used by those who keep watch until midnight; Mattins may be recited after midnight; Morning Praise and, possibly, the Noonday Prayer may be used as morning draws on. Such an extended period of adoration almost always closes with Benediction of the Blessed Sacrament.

How to Pray This Office

Before beginning this office, the first thing to remember is that Jesus in the Blessed Sacrament is truly present and hears every word we utter, silently or vocally, and every thought that crosses our minds. The second great fact is that by holy baptism we are the shrines of the Holy Spirit, who calls out without ceasing: "Abba, dear Father!" (see Mark 14:36; Romans 8:15; Galatians 4:6).

Mindful of these central theological principles, we pause for a few moments of silence before starting our prayer and recall to mind the personal presence of our Lord. The pauses that are suggested elsewhere in the text are equally helpful to fix our minds and hearts on the Host. In private recitation we may stop briefly whenever we feel called to dwell on phrases that particularly move our minds and hearts.

Each sacred text should be recited with the attention and devotion it deserves. We are addressing the Maker of the Universe and cannot afford to be casual about it! The prophets, priests, and saints who put these texts at our disposal urge us to pray both with the lips and with the heart.

People who pray alone may sit, stand, or kneel as they see fit, but they must remember that they do so in the presence of the whole court of heaven.

Prayer groups may adopt certain postures that facilitate common prayer: standing for hymns, psalms, and canticles; sitting for readings; kneeling for meditation, intercessions, and the final prayers. Change of posture is often helpful to recollection and attention.

The directions (rubrics) in Mattins apply to the rest of the hours of prayer, in both their ordinary and seasonal forms.

In the Eucharist, the Son of God comes to meet us and desires to become one with us; eucharistic adoration is simply the natural consequence of the eucharistic celebration, which is itself the church's supreme act of adoration. Receiving the Eucharist means adoring him whom we receive. Only in this way do we become one with him, and are given, as it were, a foretaste of the beauty of the heavenly liturgy. The act of adoration outside Mass prolongs and intensifies all that takes place during the liturgical celebration itself. Indeed, only in adoration can a profound and genuine reception mature. And it is precisely this personal encounter with the Lord that then strengthens the social mission contained in the Eucharist, which seeks to break down not only the walls that separate the Lord and ourselves, but also and especially the walls that separate us from one another.

Pope Benedict XVI (1927–)[53]

Mattins/Vigils

We make the sign of the cross on our lips as the
     leader says the opening versicle.

LEADER: O Lord, † open my lips,

ALL: ~AND MY MOUTH SHALL DECLARE YOUR
     PRAISE.

LEADER: My body is true food, alleluia!

ALL: ~AND MY BLOOD IS TRUE DRINK, ALLELUIA!

PSALM 100   A CALL TO PRAISE

The leader begins the antiphon to the asterisk * and
the group continues it.

He/she then recites the stanzas of Psalm 100 while
the group repeats the antiphon after each stanza.

ANTIPHON Come, let us adore Christ, * THE BREAD
     OF LIFE.

Make a joyful noise to the Lord, all you lands!
serve the Lord with gladness!
  Come into God's presence with singing!

ANTIPHON COME, LET US ADORE CHRIST, THE
     BREAD OF LIFE.

Know that the Lord , who made us, is God.
  we are the Lord's;
  we are the people of God,
  the sheep of God's pasture.

ANTIPHON COME, LET US ADORE CHRIST, THE
     BREAD OF LIFE.

Enter God's gates with thanksgiving,
   and God's courts with praise!
   Give thanks and bless God's name!

ANTIPHON: COME, LET US ADORE CHRIST, THE
      BREAD OF LIFE.

For the Lord is good;
   God's steadfast love endures for ever,
   God's faithfulness to all generations.

ANTIPHON: COME, LET US ADORE CHRIST, THE
      BREAD OF LIFE.

We bow here and at every reference to the Blessed
Trinity in this office.

Glory to the Father, and to the Son,
   and to the Holy Spirit:
as it was in the beginning, is now,
   and will be for ever. Amen.

ANTIPHON: COME, LET US ADORE CHRIST, THE
      BREAD OF LIFE.

HYMN

The leader alternates the stanzas of the hymn with
the group.

Alleluia! sing to Jesus,
His the scepter, his the throne;
Alleluia! is the triumph,
His the victory alone:
Hark! the songs of peaceful Zion
Thunder like a mighty flood;

Jesus, out of every nation,
Has redeemed us by his blood.

Alleluia! bread of angels,
You on earth our food, our stay;
Alleluia! here the sinful
Flee to you from day to day:
Intercessor, friend of sinners,
Earth's Redeemer, plead for me,
Where the songs of all the sinless
Sweep across the crystal sea.

Alleluia! King eternal,
You the Lord of lords we own;
Alleluia! born of Mary,
Earth your footstool, heaven your throne:
You within the veil have entered,
Robed in flesh, our great High Priest;
You on earth both priest and victim
In the Eucharistic feast.

William Chatterton Dix (1837–1898)

PSALM 107:1–9   GOD NOURISHES US

The leader begins the antiphon and alternates the
stanzas of the psalm with the group.

ANTIPHON Whoever comes to me will never be
hungry, * AND WHOEVER BELIEVES IN ME
WILL NEVER BE THIRSTY, ALLELUIA!

O give thanks to the Lord, who is good,
whose steadfast love endures forever!

Let the redeemed of the Lord say so,
  whom the Lord has redeemed from trouble
and gathered in from the lands,
  from the east and from the west,
  from the north and from the south.

Some wandered in the desert wastes,
  finding no way to a city in which to dwell;
hungry and thirsty,
  their soul fainted within them.

Then in their trouble, they cried to the Lord,
  who delivered them from their distress,
and led them by a straight way,
  till they reached a city in which to dwell;

Let them thank the Lord for steadfast love,
  for wonderful works to humankind.
For the Lord satisfies those who are thirsty,
  and fills the hungry with good things.

All repeat the antiphon.

ANTIPHON WHOEVER COMES TO ME WILL NEVER
      BE HUNGRY, AND WHOEVER BELIEVES IN ME
      WILL NEVER BE THIRSTY, ALLELUIA!

PSALM PRAYER

LEADER: Let us pray (pause for quiet adoration):

God our provider,
each day you furnish all our needs,
both temporal and eternal:

We put our trust in your holy promises
because, as Jesus taught us,
you are good and love the human race,
now and for ever.
ALL: ~AMEN.

MANNA FROM

READING **HEAVEN** **EXODUS 16:4–7**

READER: The LORD said to Moses, "I am going to rain bread from heaven for you, and each day the people shall go out and gather enough for that day. In that way I will test them, whether they will follow my instructions or not. On the sixth day, when they prepare what they bring in, it will be twice as much as they gather on other days." So Moses and Aaron said to all the Israelites, "In the evening you shall know that it was the LORD who brought you out of the land of Egypt, and in the morning you shall see the glory of the LORD."

Pause for Silent Adoration

RESPONSORY

LEADER: The Lord gave them bread from heaven.
ALL: ~THE LORD GAVE THEM BREAD FROM HEAVEN.

LEADER: Sending down manna for them to eat.
ALL: ~THE LORD GAVE THEM BREAD FROM HEAVEN.

An Office of the Blessed Sacrament **81**

Leader: Glory to the Father, and to the Son,
  and to the Holy Spirit.
All: ~The Lord gave them bread from
  heaven.

The Canticle of the Church

The leader alternates the stanzas of the canticle
with the group.

We praise you, O God,
we acclaim you as Lord;
all creation worships you,
the Father everlasting.

To you all angels, all the powers of heaven,
the cherubim and seraphim, sing in endless praise:

  Holy, holy, holy Lord, God of power and might,
    heaven and earth are full of your glory.

The glorious company of apostles praise you.
The noble fellowship of prophets praise you.
The white-robed army of martyrs praise you.

Throughout the world the holy church acclaims
      you:
  Father, of majesty unbounded,
  your true and only Son, worthy of all praise,
  the Holy Spirit, advocate and guide.

You, Christ, are the king of glory,
the eternal Son of the Father.

When you took our flesh to set us free
you humbly chose the Virgin's womb.

You overcame the sting of death
and opened the kingdom of heaven to all believers.
You are seated at God's right hand in glory.
We believe that you will come to be our judge.

Come, then, Lord, and help your people,
bought with the price of your own blood,
and bring us with your saints
to glory everlasting.

St. Nicetas of Remesiana (ca. 335–ca. 414)[54]

CLOSING PRAYER
LEADER: Lord Jesus Christ,
you gave us the Eucharist
as the memorial of your suffering and death.
May our worship of your sacramental body
        and blood
help us to know the salvation you won for us
and the peace that you bring to our hearts.
Your reign is a reign for all ages.
ALL: ~AMEN.

DOXOLOGY

LEADER: May the heart of Jesus in the most Blessed
Sacrament

be praised, adored, and loved, with grateful
affection,

at every moment, in all the tabernacles of the
world,

even to the end of time.

ALL: ~AMEN.

Morning Praise

We make a full sign of the cross with the opening versicle.

O God, † come to my assistance.
~O LORD, MAKE HASTE TO HELP ME.

All creatures look to you, alleluia!
~TO GIVE THEM THEIR FOODS IN DUE SEASON,
   ALLELUIA!

HYMN

Christ the king, enthroned in splendor,
Comes from heaven to be our priest!
One with him as priest and victim,
One in love, we share his feast!
Praise him in high heaven above!
Praise him in this feast of love!

Light here scatters all our darkness!
Life here triumphs over death!
Come, receive from Christ in glory
God the Spirit's living breath!
Praise Christ for his victory won!
Praise the Father's first-born Son!

Heaven is here! The gracious Father
Gives to us his only Son!
Here is sent the loving Spirit,
Making all in Christ but one!
Praise the Father, praise the Son,
Praise the Spirit, Godhead one![55]

Antiphon I come to the altar of God, *
To God, my joy, my delight.

As the deer longs for streams of water,
   so my soul longs for you, O God.
My being thirsts for God, the living God.
   When can I go and see the face of God?
My tears have been my food day and night,
   as they ask daily, "Where is your God?"

Those times I recall
   as I pour out my soul,
When I went in procession with the crowd,
   I went with them to the house of God,
Amid loud cries of thanksgiving,
   with the multitude keeping festival.

Why are you downcast, my soul;
   why do you groan within me?
Wait for God, whom I shall praise again,
   my savior and my God.

Antiphon I come to the altar of God,
To God, my joy, my delight.

Psalm Prayer

Let us pray (pause for silent adoration):

God of presence, God of power,
refresh and strengthen us with the bread of life
that we may eagerly continue our pilgrimage
and grow stronger as we travel

toward our heavenly home.
We ask this through Christ our Lord.
~Amen.

Reading   **Bread from Heaven**   **John 6:32–34**

Jesus said to them, "Very truly, I tell you, it was not
Moses who gave you the bread from heaven, but
it is my Father who gives you the true bread from
heaven. For the bread of God is that which comes
down from heaven and gives life to the world."
They said to him, "Sir, give us this bread always."

Pause for Silent Adoration

Response

Mortals ate the bread of angels, alleluia!
~God sent them food in abundance, alleluia!

The Canticle of Zachary   **Luke 1:68–79**

Antiphon How sacred is the feast*
in which Christ is our food,
the memorial of his passion is renewed,
our hearts are filled with grace,
and we receive a pledge of the glory that is
        to come, alleluia!

We make a full sign of the cross to begin the gospel
canticle.

Blessed † are you, Lord, the God of Israel,
  you have come to your people and set them free.
You have raised up for us a mighty Savior,
  born of the house of your servant David.

Through your holy prophets, you promised of old
   to save us from our enemies,
   from the hands of all who hate us,
   to show mercy to our forebears,
   and to remember your holy covenant.

This was the oath you swore to our father
      Abraham:
   to set us free from the hands of our enemies,
   free to worship you without fear,
   holy and righteous before you,
   all the days of our life.

And you, child, shall be called the prophet of the
      Most High,
   for you will go before the Lord to prepare the
      way,
to give God's people knowledge of salvation
   by the forgiveness of their sins.

In the tender compassion of our God
   the dawn from on high shall break upon us,
to shine on those who dwell in darkness
   and the shadow of death,
   and to guide our feet into the way of peace.

Glory to the Holy and Undivided Trinity:
now and always and for ever and ever. Amen.

Antiphon How sacred is the feast
in which Christ is our food,
the memorial of his passion is renewed,
our hearts are filled with grace,

AND WE RECEIVE A PLEDGE OF THE GLORY THAT IS
TO COME, ALLELUIA!

THE LORD'S PRAYER

Lord, have mercy.

~CHRIST, HAVE MERCY. LORD, HAVE MERCY.

Our Father in heaven, (all in unison):

CLOSING PRAYER

Lord Jesus Christ,
you gave us the Eucharist
as the memorial of your suffering and death.
May our worship of this sacrament
of your body and blood
help us to know the salvation you won for us
and the peace of your kingdom,
where you live with the Father and the Holy Spirit,
one God, for ever and ever.

~AMEN.[56]

DOXOLOGY

May the heart of Jesus in the Most Blessed
      Sacrament
be praised, adored, and loved, with grateful
      affection,
at every moment, in all the tabernacles of the
      world,
even to the end of time.

~AMEN.

Noonday Prayer

We make a full sign of the cross with the opening versicle.

Help me ✝ speak, Lord,
~AND I WILL PRAISE YOU.

Take and eat; this is my body broken for you,
    alleluia!
~TAKE AND DRINK; THIS IS THE CUP OF
    SALVATION, ALLELUIA!

Hymn

Let all mortal flesh keep silence,
And with fear and trembling stand;
Ponder nothing earthly minded,
For with blessing in his hand
Christ our God to earth descendeth,
Our full homage to demand.

King of kings, yet born of Mary,
As of old on earth he stood,
Lord of lords in human vesture,
In the Body and the Blood
He will give to all the faithful
His own self for heavenly food.

Rank on rank the host of heaven
Spreads its vanguard on the way,
As the Light of Light descendeth
From the realms of endless day,

That the powers of hell may vanish
As the darkness clears away.

At his feet the six-winged seraph;
Cherubim with sleepless eye,
Veil their faces to the Presence,
As with ceaseless voice they cry,
"Alleluia, Alleluia,
Alleluia, Lord Most High!"[57]

A CANTICLE OF
ISAIAH THE PROPHET   ISAIAH 49:8–13 NAB

ANTIPHON I am the living bread * THAT CAME
    DOWN FROM HEAVEN. IF YOU EAT THIS
    BREAD, YOU WILL LIVE FOR EVER, ALLELUIA!

In a time of favor I answer you,
  on the day of salvation I help you,
to restore the land
  and allot the desolate heritages,
saying to the prisoners: Come out!
To those in darkness:
  Show yourselves!

Along the paths they shall find pasture,
  on every bare height shall their pastures be.
They shall not hunger or thirst,
  nor shall the scorching wind or the sun strike
    them;
For he who pities them leads them
  and guides them beside springs of water.

I will cut a road through all my mountains,
  and make my highway level.
See, some shall come from afar,
  others from the north and the west,
  and some from the land of Syene.

Sing out, O heavens, and rejoice, O earth,
  break into song, you mountains.
For the LORD comforts his people
  and shows mercy to the afflicted.

ANTIPHON I AM THE LIVING BREAD THAT CAME
DOWN FROM HEAVEN. IF YOU EAT THIS
BREAD, YOU WILL LIVE FOR EVER, ALLELUIA!

PSALM PRAYER
Let us pray (pause for quiet adoration):

Jesus, Servant of the Lord,
on the day of salvation,
we will break into song
because you take away our hunger
and quench our thirst
with your own body and blood.
Your reign is a reign for all ages.
~AMEN.

READING   **BREAD FROM HEAVEN**   **JOHN 6:48–51**
Jesus said to them, "I am the bread of life. Your
ancestors ate the manna in the wilderness, and
they died. This is the bread that comes down from
heaven, so that one may eat of it and not die. I am

the living bread that came down from heaven.
Whoever eats of this bread will live forever; and
the bread that I will give for the life of the world is
my flesh."

Pause for Silent Adoration

RESPONSE

Do not work for the food that perishes, alleluia!
~BUT FOR THE FOOD THAT ENDURES FOR
    ETERNAL LIFE, ALLELUIA!

CLOSING PRAYER

Lord Jesus Christ,
we worship you living among us
in the sacrament of your body and blood.
May we offer to our Father in heaven
a solemn pledge of undivided love.
May we offer to our brothers and sisters
a life poured out in loving service of the kingdom
where you live with the Father,
in the unity of the Holy Spirit,
one God, for ever and ever.
~AMEN.[58]

Let us bless the Lord.
~THANKS BE TO GOD.

Evening Prayer

We make a full sign of the cross with the opening versicle.

Jesus Christ † is the light of the world.
~A LIGHT NO DARKNESS CAN EXTINGUISH.

Very truly, I tell you, alleluia!
~WHOEVER BELIEVES HAS ETERNAL LIFE,
ALLELUIA!

Hymn

Jesus, Lord of glory, clothed in heaven's light,
Here I bow before you, hidden from my sight.
King to whom my body, mind and heart belong,
Mind and heart here falter, love so deep, so strong.

Here distrust, my spirit, eye and tongue and hand,
Trust faith's ear and listen, hear and understand.
Hear the voice of Wisdom, speaking now to you;
When God's Word has spoken, what can be more
     true?

Once you hid your glory, Jesus crucified;
Now you hide your body, Jesus glorified.
When you come in judgment, plain for all to see,
God and man in splendor; Lord, remember me.

Once you showed to Thomas wounded hands and
     side;
Here I kneel adoring, faith alone my guide.

Help me grow in faith, Lord, grow in hope and
    love,
Living by your Spirit, gift of God above.

Here I see your dying, Jesus, victim-priest;
Here I know your rising, host and guest and feast.
Let me taste your goodness, manna from the
    skies;
Feed me, heal me, save me, food of Paradise.

Heart of Jesus, broken, pierced, and opened wide,
Wash me in the water flowing from your side.
Jesus' blood, so precious that one drop could free
All the world from evil, come and ransom me.

How I long to see you, Jesus, face to face
How my heart is thirsting, living spring of grace.
Show me soon your glory, be my great reward,
Be my joy for ever, Jesus, gracious Lord. Amen.

Attributed to St. Thomas Aquinas (1225-1279)[59]

PSALM 23   JESUS, SHEPHERD AND HOST

ANTIPHON I am the good shepherd; * I KNOW MINE
AND MINE KNOW ME.

The Lord is my shepherd, I shall not want;
  the Lord makes me lie down in green pastures,
leads me beside still waters;
  restores my life,
leads me in right paths
  for the sake of the Lord's name.

Even though I walk through the darkest valley,
  I fear no evil;
for you are with me
  your rod and your staff,
  they comfort me.

You prepare a table before me
  in the presence of my enemies;
you anoint my head with oil,
  my cup overflows.

Only goodness and mercy shall follow me
  all the days of my life;
And I shall dwell in the house of the Lord
  as long as I live.

ANTIPHON I AM THE GOOD SHEPHERD; I KNOW
        MINE AND MINE KNOW ME.

PSALM PRAYER
Let us pray (pause for quiet adoration):

Lord Jesus Christ,
in the wonderful sacrament of the altar
you provide a living memorial banquet for us
and an everlasting covenant in your blood.
Keep us ever mindful of your protection
and faithful to your commandment of love,
now and for ever.
~AMEN.

READING   **1 Corinthians**
The Lord's Supper   **11:23–26**

I received from the Lord what I also handed on
to you, that the Lord Jesus on the night he was
betrayed took a loaf of bread, and when he had
given thanks, he broke it and said, "This my body
that is broken for you. Do this in remembrance of
me." In the same way he took the cup also, after
supper, saying, "This cup is the new Covenant
in my blood. Do this, as often as you drink it, in
remembrance of me."

Pause for Silent Adoration

RESPONSE
As often as you eat this bread and drink the cup,
~You proclaim the Lord's death until he
    comes.

The Canticle of the Virgin Mary   **Luke 1:46–55**

Antiphon How sacred is the feast *
in which Christ is our food,
the memorial of his passion is renewed,
our hearts are filled with grace,
and we receive a pledge of the glory that is
    to come, alleluia!

We make a full sign of the cross to begin the gospel
canticle.

My soul † proclaims the greatness of the Lord,
my spirit rejoices in God my Savior,
for you, Lord, have looked with favor on your
     lowly servant.

From this day all generations will call me blessed:
  you, the Almighty, have done great things for me
  and holy is your name.
  You have mercy on those who fear you,
  from generation to generation.

You have shown strength with your arm
and scattered the proud in their conceit,
casting down the mighty from their thrones
and lifting up the lowly.
You have filled the hungry with good things
and sent the rich away empty.

You have come to the aid of your servant Israel,
to remember the promise of mercy,
the promise made to our forebears,
to Abraham and his children for ever.

To the Ruler of the ages,
immortal, invisible, the only wise God,
be honor and glory, through Jesus Christ,
for ever and ever. Amen.

ANTIPHON HOW SACRED IS THE FEAST
IN WHICH CHRIST IS OUR FOOD,
THE MEMORIAL OF HIS PASSION IS RENEWED,

OUR HEARTS ARE FILLED WITH GRACE,
AND WE RECEIVE A PLEDGE OF THE GLORY THAT IS
TO COME, ALLELUIA!

A LITANY OF THE BLESSED SACRAMENT
(see pages 40–42)

PRAYER

Lord Jesus Christ,
you gave us the Eucharist
as the memorial of your suffering and death.
May our worship of this sacrament
of your body and blood
help us to experience the salvation you won for us
and the peace of your kingdom,
where you live with the Father,
in the unity of the Holy Spirit,
one God, for ever and ever.
~AMEN.

DOXOLOGY

May the heart of Jesus in the Most Blessed
Sacrament
be praised, adored, and loved, with grateful
affection,
at every moment, in all the tabernacles of the
world,
even to the end of time.
~AMEN.

Night Prayer/Compline

We make a full sign of the cross with the opening versicle.

Our help † is in the name of the Lord,
~THE MAKER OF HEAVEN AND EARTH.

You gave your people food of angels,
~AND SUPPLIED THEM WITH BREAD READY TO
    EAT.

HYMN

Christ gives his children angels' food,
His body and his blood divine;
The poor receive a priceless gift:
Strong bread of life, immortal wine.

There is no other bread than this
By which the hungry can be filled;
No other wine has hidden power
Whereby the spirit's thirst is stilled.

All those who have believed his word,
All share, in love, this holy bread,
Who drink together from this cup,
Christ will not leave among the dead.

To all rejoicing at this feast,
Death opens doors on realms of light,
Where Father, Son, and Spirit reign,
And we attain immortal life. Amen.[60]

ANTIPHON Lift up * THE LIGHT OF YOUR
       COUNTENANCE UPON US, O LORD!

Answer me when I call, O God of my right!
   You have given me room when I was in distress.
   Be gracious to me, and hear my prayer.

How long, O people, shall my honor suffer shame?
   How long will you love emptiness, and seek after
      lies?
But know that the Lord has set apart the faithful;
   the Lord hears when I call.

Be angry, but do not sin;
   commune with your own hearts on your beds,
   and be silent.
Offer right sacrifices,
   and put your trust in the Lord.

There are many who say,
    "O that we might see some good!
    Lift up the light of your countenance upon us,
       O Lord!"
You have put more joy in my heart
   than have their grain and wine.

In peace I will both lie down and sleep,
   for you alone, O Lord, make me lie down in
      safety.

ANTIPHON LIFT UP THE LIGHT OF YOUR
       COUNTENANCE UPON US, O LORD!

PSALM PRAYER

Let us pray (pause for quiet adoration):

Lord Jesus Christ,
you longed to eat the last supper with your
    disciples
to prepare them for the paschal mystery:
By the beauty of your sacrificial meal,
may we rejoice with all Christian believers
who die and rise in you and for you.
Your live and reign for all ages.
~Amen.

READING   EATING AND DRINKING   JOHN 6:53–56

Jesus said to them: "Very truly, I tell you, unless you eat the flesh of the Son of Man and drink his blood, you have no life in you. Those who eat my flesh and drink my blood have eternal life, and I will raise them up on the last day; for my flesh is true food and my blood is true drink. Those who eat my flesh and drink my blood abide in me, and I in them."

Pause for Silent Adoration

RESPONSE

We have come to believe and know, alleluia!
~THAT YOU ARE THE HOLY ONE OF GOD,
    ALLELUIA!

THE CANTICLE OF SIMEON   LUKE 2:29–32

We make a full sign of the cross to begin the gospel canticle.

ANTIPHON This is the bread * THAT CAME DOWN
FROM HEAVEN, ALLELUIA!

Now, Lord, † you let your servant go in peace
 your word has been fulfilled.

My own eyes have seen the salvation
 which you have prepared in the sight of every
        people:
a light to reveal you to the nation
 and the glory of your people Israel.

Glory to the Father, and to the Son,
 and to the Holy Spirit:
as it was in the beginning, is now,
  and will be for ever. Amen.

ANTIPHON THIS IS THE BREAD THAT CAME DOWN
FROM HEAVEN, ALLELUIA!

CLOSING PRAYER
Be present, be present, O Jesus,
great and good High Priest:
Be present to us as you were
to your disciples at the last supper
and as you were made known
in the opening of the scriptures
and in the breaking of bread
at Emmaus on Easter evening.
Your reign is a reign for all ages.
~AMEN.

DOXOLOGY

May the heart of Jesus in the Most Blessed
    Sacrament
be praised, adored, and loved, with grateful
    affection,
at every moment, in all the tabernacles of the
    world,
even to the end of time.

~AMEN.

Benediction of the Blessed Sacrament

At *public* celebrations of this office, Benediction
of the Blessed Sacrament is usually observed at its
close.

HYMN: *TANTUM ERGO*

This hymn and its prayer are sung kneeling just
before the Benediction.

Come, adore this wondrous presence;
Bow to Christ, the source of grace!
Here is kept the ancient promise
Of God's earthly dwelling place!
Sight is blind before God's glory,
Faith alone may see his face!

Glory be to God the Father,
Praise to his co-equal Son,
Adoration to the Spirit,
Bond of love, in Godhead one!

Blest be God by all creation
Joyously while ages run![61]

LEADER: You gave them bread from heaven
ALL: ~AND THIS BREAD CONTAINED ALL
GOODNESS.

Let us pray:

LEADER: Lord Jesus Christ
you gave us the Eucharist
as the memorial of your suffering and death.
May our worship of this sacrament of your body
and blood
help us to experience the salvation you won for us
and the peace of the kingdom
where you live with the Father,
in the unity of the Holy Spirit,
one God, for ever and ever.
ALL: ~AMEN.

The priest assumes the humeral veil, takes up the
ciborium or monstrance, and makes the sign of the
cross over the assembly.

THE DIVINE PRAISES

This set of praises is often used after Benediction
of the Blessed Sacrament and is also very useful for
private prayer.

Blessed be God.
Blessed be his Holy Name.
Blessed be Jesus Christ, true God and true Man.

Blessed be the Name of Jesus.
Blessed be his most Sacred Heart.
Blessed be his most Precious Blood.
Blessed be Jesus in the most Holy Sacrament of
     the Altar.
Blessed be the Holy Spirit, the Paraclete.
Blessed be the great Mother of God, Mary most
     holy.
Blessed be her holy and Immaculate Conception.
Blessed be her glorious Assumption.
Blessed be the name of Mary, Virgin and Mother.
Blessed be Saint Joseph, her most chaste spouse.
Blessed be God in his angels and in his saints.
~Amen.

Psalm 117   Call to Praise

This psalm usually brings Benediction to a close.

Praise the Lord, all you nations!
  Give glory, all you peoples!
The Lord's love for us is strong;
  the Lord is faithful forever.

Glory to the Father, and to the Son,
  and to the Holy Spirit:
as it was in the beginning, is now,
  and will be for ever. Amen.

DOXOLOGY

May the heart of Jesus in the Most Blessed
     Sacrament
be praised, adored, and loved, with grateful
     affection,
at every moment, in all the tabernacles of the
     world,
even to the end of time.

ALL: ~AMEN.

Part 3
Holy Hours for Eucharistic Adoration

The Church and the world have a great need for Eucharistic worship. Jesus awaits us in this sacrament of love. Let us not refuse the time to go to meet him in adoration, in contemplation full of faith, and open to making amends for the serious offenses and crimes of the world. Let our adoration never cease.

Pope John Paul II (1920–2005)[62]

Holy Hours in honor of the Blessed Sacrament may take place before the tabernacle or ciborium or before a monstrance displaying the reserved sacrament. Such devotions may be part of the Forty Hours, the feast of Corpus Christi, Nocturnal Adoration exercises, perpetual adoration, or privately at any time. Homebound persons are encouraged to make holy hours at home while turning their attention to the tabernacle of their parish church.

Holy Hours have no official format but are usually composed of hymns and/or psalms, readings from Scripture, a meditation or brief sermon, silent prayer, an act of dedication, intercessions, and, finally, Benediction of the Blessed Sacrament when the Holy Hour is celebrated publicly.

A Holy Hour Before the Blessed Sacrament

The following example might be considered typical for either a public or private observance.

   The pauses for silent prayer should last for several minutes to permit and encourage more personal adoration of the Blessed Sacrament.

We make a full sign of the cross with the opening versicle.

LEADER: In the name † of the Father, and of the Son, and of the Holy Spirit.

ALL: ~AMEN.

LEADER: Blessed be Jesus in the Most Holy Sacrament of the altar!

ALL: ~BLESSED BE THE NAME OF JESUS, NOW AND FOR EVER! AMEN.

PSALM 67   AN INVITATION TO PRAISE AND PRAYER

The leader begins the antiphon and the group continues it. He/she then recites the stanzas of Psalm 100 while the group repeats the antiphon after each stanza.

ANTIPHON Come, let us adore Christ the Lord, the bread of life. * COME, LET US ADORE HIM!

O God, be gracious to us and bless us
   and make your face shine upon us,

that your way may be known upon earth,
  and your saving power among all nations.
Let the peoples praise you, O God,
  let all the peoples praise you!

ANTIPHON COME, LET US ADORE CHRIST THE
      LORD, THE BREAD OF LIFE. COME, LET US
      ADORE HIM!

Let the nations be glad and sing for joy,
  for you judge the peoples with equity
  and guide the nations upon earth.
Let the peoples praise you, O God,
  let all the peoples praise you!

ANTIPHON COME, LET US ADORE CHRIST THE
      LORD, THE BREAD OF LIFE. COME, LET US
      ADORE HIM!

The earth has yielded its increase;
  God, our God has blessed us.
May God bless us;
  let all the ends of the earth fear God!

ANTIPHON COME, LET US ADORE CHRIST THE
      LORD, THE BREAD OF LIFE. COME, LET US
      ADORE HIM!

Glory to the Father, and to the Son,
  and to the Holy Spirit:
as it was in the beginning, is now,
  and will be for ever. Amen.

ANTIPHON COME, LET US ADORE CHRIST THE
LORD, THE BREAD OF LIFE. COME, LET US
ADORE HIM!

The leader alternates the stanzas of the hymn with
the group.

EUCHARISTIC HYMN

O Jesus, joy of loving hearts,
The fount of life and our true light,
We seek the peace your love imparts
And stand rejoicing in your sight.

Your truth unchanged has ever stood;
You save all those who heed your call;
To those who seek you, you are good,
To those who find you, all in all.

We taste you, Lord, our living bread,
And long to feast upon you still;
We drink of you, the fountain-head,
Our thirsting souls to quench and fill.

For you our restless spirit yearns,
Where'er our changing lot is cast;
Glad, when your presence we discern,
Blest when our faith can hold you fast.

O Jesus, with us ever stay;
Make all our moments calm and bright;
Oh, chase the night of sin away,
Shed o'er the world your holy light.

St. Bernard of Clairvaux (1091–1153)[63]

We pray Psalm 111 and/or Psalm 84.

PSALM 111   **CHRIST'S MEMORIAL MEAL**

The leader begins the antiphon, all continue it, and the leader alternates the stanzas of the psalm with the group.

ANTIPHON The Lord provides food * FOR THOSE
WHO ARE FAITHFUL AND IS EVER MINDFUL
OF THE COVENANT.

I will give thanks to the Lord with my whole
        heart,
  in the company of the upright, in the
        congregation.
Great are the works of the Lord,
  studied by all who delight in them.

Full of honor and majesty are the works of the
        Lord
  whose righteousness endures forever,
who has given us a memory of these wonderful
        works;
  the Lord is gracious and merciful.
The Lord provides food for those who are faithful
  and is ever mindful of the covenant.

The Lord has shown God's people the power of
        these works;
  by giving them the heritage of the nations.
The works of the Lord's hands are faithful and just;
  the precepts of the Lord are trustworthy;

they are established forever and ever,
  to be performed with faithfulness and
      uprightness.

The Lord sent redemption to his people;
  and has commanded the covenant forever.
  Holy and wondrous is God's name!
The fear of the Lord is the beginning of wisdom;
  all those who practice it have a good
      understanding.
  The praise of the Lord endures for ever.

All repeat the antiphon in unison.

ANTIPHON THE LORD PROVIDES FOOD FOR THOSE
          WHO ARE FAITHFUL AND IS EVER MINDFUL
          OF THE COVENANT.

PSALM PRAYER
LEADER: Let us pray (pause for quiet adoration):

Lord Jesus Christ,
in the wonderful Sacrament of the Altar
you provide a living memorial of your dying and
      rising
and of the everlasting covenant in your blood.
Keep us ever mindful of all your wonderful works
and especially of your perpetual presence in our
      tabernacles.
You live and reign for ever and ever.
ALL: ~AMEN.

The leader begins the antiphon, all continue it, and
the leader alternates the stanzas of the psalm with
the group.

ANTIPHON How lovely is your dwelling place, * O
     LORD OF HOSTS!

My soul longs, indeed it faints
   for the courts of the Lord;
my heart and flesh sing for joy to the living God.

O Lord of hosts, my Ruler and my God,
   at your altars even the sparrow finds a home,
   and the swallow a nest for herself,
   where she may lay her young.

Blessed are those who dwell in your house,
   ever singing your praise!
Blessed are those whose strength is in you,
   in whose heart are the highways to Zion.

As they go through the valley of tears,
   they make it a place of springs;
   the early rain also covers it with pools.
They go from strength to strength;
   the God of gods will be seen in Zion.

O Lord of hosts, hear my prayer;
   O God of Jacob, hear!
Behold our shield, O God;
   look upon the face of your anointed!

For a day in your courts is better
  than a thousand elsewhere.
I would rather be a doorkeeper in the house of my
      God
  than dwell in the tents of wickedness.

For the Lord God is a sun and a shield,
  and bestows favor and honor.
O Lord of hosts,
  blessed are they who trust in you!

All repeat the antiphon in unison.

ANTIPHON HOW LOVELY IS YOUR DWELLING PLACE,
O LORD OF HOSTS!

PSALM PRAYER

LEADER: Let us pray (pause for quiet adoration):

Lord God of hosts,
look upon the face of your Anointed,
the face of Jesus, your Messiah,
who resides in our tabernacles
for the refreshment and the joy of your people.
His reign is a reign for all ages.

ALL: ~AMEN.

1 CORINTHIANS
READING   **THE LORD'S SUPPER**   **11:23–26**
READER: I received from the Lord what I also
handed on to you, that the Lord Jesus on the
night he was betrayed took a loaf of bread, and
when he had given thanks, he broke it and said,

"This my body that is broken for you. Do this in remembrance of me." In the same way he took the cup also, after supper, saying, "This cup is the new Covenant in my blood. Do this, as often as you drink it, in remembrance of me."

(Meditation or Sermon on the Blessed Sacrament)

Pause for Silent Adoration

RESPONSE

LEADER: As often as you eat this bread and drink this cup,

ALL: ~YOU PROCLAIM THE DEATH OF THE LORD UNTIL HE COMES.

THE CANTICLE OF THE VIRGIN MARY   LUKE 1:46–55

The leader begins the antiphon and all continue it.

ANTIPHON How sacred is the feast *
IN WHICH CHRIST IS OUR FOOD,
THE MEMORIAL OF HIS PASSION IS RENEWED,
OUR HEARTS ARE FILLED WITH GRACE,
AND WE RECEIVE A PLEDGE OF THE GLORY THAT IS
    TO COME, ALLELUIA!

All make the sign of the cross to open the gospel canticle. The leader alternates the stanzas of Mary's canticle with the group.

My soul † proclaims the greatness of the Lord,
my spirit rejoices in God my Savior,
for you, Lord, have looked with favor on your
    lowly servant.

From this day all generations will call me blessed:
you, the Almighty, have done great things for me
and holy is your name.
You have mercy on those who fear you,
from generation to generation.

You have shown strength with your arm
and scattered the proud in their conceit,
casting down the mighty from their thrones
and lifting up the lowly.
You have filled the hungry with good things
and sent the rich away empty.

You have come to the aid of your servant Israel,
to remember the promise of mercy,
the promise made to our forebears,
to Abraham and his children for ever.

To the Ruler of the ages,
immortal, invisible, the only wise God,
be honor and glory, through Jesus Christ,
for ever and ever. Amen.

All repeat the antiphon in unison.

ANTIPHON HOW SACRED IS THE FEAST
IN WHICH CHRIST IS OUR FOOD,
THE MEMORIAL OF HIS PASSION IS RENEWED,
OUR HEARTS ARE FILLED WITH GRACE,
AND WE RECEIVE A PLEDGE OF THE GLORY THAT IS
TO COME, ALLELUIA!

Act of Dedication to Christ the King

The leader recites each section of this act and all respond with the refrain.

Loving Jesus, Redeemer of the world,
we are yours, and yours we wish to be.
To bind ourselves to you even more closely
we kneel before you today
and offer ourselves to your most Sacred Heart.

ALL: ~PRAISE TO YOU, OUR SAVIOR AND OUR KING.

Have mercy on all who have never known you
and on all who reject you and refuse to obey you:
gentle Lord, draw them to yourself.

ALL: ~PRAISE TO YOU, OUR SAVIOR AND OUR KING.

Reign over the faithful who have never left you,
reign over those who have squandered their
        inheritance,
the prodigal children who now are starving:
bring them back to their Father's house.

ALL: ~PRAISE TO YOU, OUR SAVIOR AND OUR KING.

Reign over those who are misled by error or
        divided by discord.
Hasten the day when we shall be one in faith and
        truth,
one flock with you, the one Shepherd.
Give to your Church freedom and peace,
and to all nations justice and order.

ALL: ~PRAISE TO YOU, OUR SAVIOR AND OUR KING.

Make the earth resound from pole to pole with a
      single cry:
Praise to the Divine Heart that gained our
      salvation;
glory and honor be his for ever and ever. Amen.

ALL: ~PRAISE TO YOU, OUR SAVIOR AND OUR
      KING.[64]

A LITANY OF THE BLESSED SACRAMENT
(see pages 40–42)

DOXOLOGY

May the heart of Jesus in the Most Blessed
      Sacrament
be praised, adored, and loved, with grateful
      affection,
at every moment, in all the tabernacles of the
      world,
even to the end of time.

ALL: ~AMEN.

A *public* Holy Hour always concludes with
Benediction of the Blessed Sacrament. See pages
104–106.

A Holy Hour to the
Sacred Heart of Jesus

As devotion to the five wounds of Jesus grew more and more intense in the High Middle Ages, it tended to concentrate on the wound in his side and then, more and more, on the broken and pierced Heart that lay within. Two medieval nuns, spiritual writers of first rank, Mechtild of Hackeborn (1241–1298) and Gertrude the Great (1256–1302) are usually considered the founders of the devotion to the Sacred Heart of Jesus. In seventeenth-century France, devotion to the Sacred Heart grew rapidly under the influence of the mystic St. Margaret Mary Alacoque (1647–1690). It was embraced and spread in a particular way by the Company of Jesus and by other apostles of the Sacred Heart. This special devotion gave rise to the practice of the Nine First Fridays, the Holy Hour of Adoration before the Blessed Sacrament, the feast and Mass of the Sacred Heart, and to the dedication of families to the Sacred Heart of Jesus.

Let us kneel in worship before the crucified Jesus, still bearing his five wounds in his resurrected body and really present in the Blessed Sacrament of the Altar.

The rubrics (directions) for this Holy Hour are the same as those in the Holy Hour of the Blessed Sacrament, pages 111–121.

Blood and Water
So that the Church might be drawn from Christ's side as he slept on the cross and in order to fulfill the Scripture, "They will look on the one whom

they have pierced"(John 19:37), God permitted one of the soldiers to pierce his side with a spear. As blood and water poured forth from his sacred side, the price of our salvation gushing from his Heart empowered the Church's sacraments to award us the life of grace and to confer on those already living in Christ a draught of the living "spring of water gushing up to eternal life" (John 4:14).

St. Bonaventure (1217–1274)[65]

O Lord, † open my lips,
~AND MY MOUTH WILL DECLARE YOUR PRAISE.
When I am lifted up,
~I WILL DRAW ALL THINGS TO MYSELF.

PSALM 95:1–7   AN INVITATION TO PRAISE AND PRAYER

ANTIPHON Come, let us worship the Heart of Jesus,
* PIERCED BY A SPEAR FOR LOVE OF US,
ALLELUIA!

O come, let us sing to the Lord;
let us make a joyful noise
to the rock of our salvation!
Let us come into God's presence with
thanksgiving;
let us make a joyful noise with songs of praise!

ANTIPHON COME, LET US WORSHIP THE HEART OF
JESUS, PIERCED BY A SPEAR FOR LOVE OF US,
ALLELUIA!

For the Lord is a great God,
  and a great Ruler above all gods,
in whose hands are the depths of the earth
  and also the heights of the mountains.
The sea belongs to God who made it,
  and the dry land, because God formed it.

ANTIPHON COME, LET US WORSHIP THE HEART OF
  JESUS, PIERCED BY A SPEAR FOR LOVE OF US,
  ALLELUIA!

O come, let us worship and bow down,
  let us kneel before the Lord, our Maker!
For the Lord is our God,
  we are the people of God's pasture,
  the sheep of God's hand.
Hear the voice of the Lord today!

ANTIPHON COME, LET US WORSHIP THE HEART OF
  JESUS, PIERCED BY A SPEAR FOR LOVE OF US,
  ALLELUIA!

Glory to the Father, and to the Son,
  and to the Holy Spirit:
as it was in the beginning, is now,
  and will be for ever. Amen.

ANTIPHON COME, LET US WORSHIP THE HEART OF
  JESUS, PIERCED BY A SPEAR FOR LOVE OF US,
  ALLELUIA!

HYMN TO THE SACRED HEART OF JESUS

The love of God is shown to all
In Christ our Savior's wounded heart;
He asks us now to share his cross
And in his passion take our part.

We are the Father's gift to Christ
Who loved his own until the end;
His burden light we bear with joy,
And gladly to his yoke we bend.

Where love and loving-kindness are,
The God of love will always be:
With cords of love he binds us fast,
Yet leaves the willing captive free.

Praise Father, Son, and Spirit blest,
Eternal Trinity sublime,
Who make their home in humble hearts,
Indwelling to the end of time.[66]

PSALM 36:6–12   THE LOVE OF GOD NAB

ANTIPHON How precious * IS YOUR LOVE, O GOD!

Lord, your love reaches to heaven;
  your fidelity, to the clouds.
Your justice is like the highest mountains;
  your judgments, like the mighty deep;
  all living creatures you sustain, LORD.

How precious is your love, O God!
  We take refuge in the shadow of your wings.

We feast on the rich food of your house;
   from your delightful stream you give us drink.

For with you is the fountain of life,
   and in your light we see light.
Continue your kindness toward your friends,
   your just defense of the honest heart.
Do not let the foot of the proud overtake me,
   nor the hand of the wicked disturb me.

ANTIPHON HOW PRECIOUS IS YOUR LOVE, O GOD!

PSALM PRAYER
Let us pray (pause for silent adoration):

Heavenly Father,
be pleased to grant us
the gift of profound reverence
for the Sacred Heart of Jesus,
pierced for us on the cross.
By his sacrificial gift of himself,
make us more and more aware
of his total love for us
in the Blessed Sacrament of the Altar.
We ask this through the same Christ our Lord.
~AMEN.

READING   **THE PIERCING OF HIS HEART**   JOHN 19:32–37
The soldiers came and broke the legs of the
first [criminal] and of the other who had been
crucified with him. But when they came to Jesus

and saw that he was already dead, they did not break his legs. Instead, one of the soldiers pierced his side with a spear, and at once blood and water came out. These things occurred so that the scripture might be fulfilled, "None of his bones shall be broken." And again another passage of scripture says, "They will look on the one they have pierced."

Pause for Silent Adoration

RESPONSE

My yoke is easy, alleluia!
~AND MY BURDEN IS LIGHT, ALLELUIA!

THE CANTICLE OF ISAIAH THE PROPHET 12:2–6

ANTIPHON We are saved * BY GRACE THROUGH FAITH, ALLELUIA!

Surely God is my salvation;
  I will trust, and will not be afraid,
for the LORD God is my strength and my might;
  he has become my salvation.

With joy you will draw water
  from the wells of salvation.
And you will say in that day:
  Give thanks to the LORD,
  call on his name;
make known his deeds among the nations;
  proclaim that his name is exalted.

Sing praises to the L ORD,
    for he has done gloriously;
    let this be known in all the earth.
Shout aloud and sing for joy, O royal Zion,
    for great in your midst is the Holy One of Israel.

To the Ruler of the ages, immortal, invisible,
    the only wise God,
be honor and glory, through Jesus Christ,
    for ever and ever. Amen.

A NTIPHON W E ARE SAVED BY GRACE THROUGH
        FAITH, ALLELUIA!

Act of Dedication to the Sacred Heart of Jesus

The leader recites each section of this prayer and all respond with the refrain.

Loving Jesus, Redeemer of the world,
we are yours, and yours we wish to be.
To bind ourselves to you even more closely
we kneel before you today
and offer ourselves to your most Sacred Heart.

A LL: **~P RAISE TO YOU, OUR SAVIOR AND OUR KING.**

Have mercy on all who have never known you
and on all who reject you and refuse to obey you:
gentle Lord, draw them to yourself.

A LL: **~P RAISE TO YOU, OUR SAVIOR AND OUR KING.**

Reign over the faithful who have never left you,
reign over those who have squandered their
    inheritance,
the prodigal children who now are starving:
bring them back to their Father's house.

ALL: ~PRAISE TO YOU, OUR SAVIOR AND OUR KING.

Reign over those who are misled by error or
    divided by discord.
Hasten the day when we shall be one in faith and
    truth,
one flock with you, the one Shepherd.
Give to your Church freedom and peace,
and to all nations justice and order.

ALL: ~PRAISE TO YOU, OUR SAVIOR AND OUR KING.

Make the earth resound from pole to pole with a
    single cry:
Praise to the Divine Heart that gained our
    salvation;
glory and honor be his for ever and ever. Amen.

ALL: ~PRAISE TO YOU, OUR SAVIOR AND OUR KING.

THE LITANY OF THE SACRED HEART
(see pages 226–229)

THE LORD'S PRAYER
Lord, have mercy.
~CHRIST, HAVE MERCY. LORD, HAVE MERCY.
Our Father in heaven, (all in unison) . . .

CLOSING PRAYER

Father,

we have wounded the heart of Jesus your Son,

but he brings us forgiveness and grace.

Help us to prove our grateful love

and make amends for our sins.

We ask this through our Lord Jesus Christ, your
    Son,

who lives and reigns with you,

in the unity of the Holy Spirit,

one God, for ever and ever.

~AMEN.[67]

DOXOLOGY

May the heart of Jesus in the Most Blessed
    Sacrament

be praised, adored, and loved, with grateful
    affection,

at every moment, in all the tabernacles of the
    world,

even to the end of time.

~AMEN.

A *public* Holy Hour always concludes with
Benediction of the Blessed Sacrament. See pages
104–106.

Holy Hours for the
Special Seasons

The Liturgy is not just a mental commemoration
of past events; they are present, saving events in
the sacraments of a worshipping Church. What
we could see in our Redeemer while he was on
earth has now passed over into sacraments.

St. Leo the Great (✝ 461)[68]

The previous Holy Hours before the Blessed Sacrament
are for the Ordinary Season throughout the year. The
special seasons have their particular value by connect-
ing us to the even more striking parts of the Church's
year of grace. This is especially true when we pray these
Holy Hours before Jesus in the Blessed Sacrament.

The rubrics (directions) for these holy hours are the
same as those in the previous Holy Hours before
the Blessed Sacrament, pages 111–121.

A Holy Hour for the Season of Advent

The season of Advent is roughly four weeks long;
it begins on the Sunday on or nearest the feast of
St. Andrew the Apostle (November 30) and lasts until
Christmas Eve. It is a special preparation for the season of Christmas and its splendid manifestations that
not only ready us for the first coming of Jesus into the
world but also for his great return at the end of time.

Advent is a season of comings, arrivals, and
encounters:

John the Baptist appears as the herald of the coming Messiah, preaching repentance, conversion, and baptism in the River Jordan (Mark 1:1–11).

The Archangel Gabriel comes as a messenger of the Most High to Mary of Nazareth and asks her to accept in faith the mission and destiny of being the mother of the Messiah (Luke 1:26–38).

An angel of the Lord appears to Joseph, Mary's betrothed, in a dream, and tells him not to be afraid to take an already pregnant Mary as his bride (Matthew 1:18–23).

In this season marked by such Scriptural anticipation, we await in expectant awe for the birth of Jesus, for his manifestation to the shepherds and the magi, for his revelation to the two ancients, Simeon and Anna, and, finally, for his baptism by John in the Jordan and the beginning of the Messianic era.

The pauses for silent prayer should last for several minutes of adoration.

Light and peace † in Jesus Christ our Lord.
~THANKS BE TO GOD.
Hosanna to the Son of David!
~HOSANNA IN THE HIGHEST!

HYMN

O Child of promise, come!
O come, Emmanuel!
Come, prince of peace to David's throne;
Come, God, with us to dwell!

The Lord's true servant, come,
In whom is his delight,

On whom his Holy Spirit rests,
The Gentiles' promised light.

O come, anointed One,
To show blind eyes your face!
Good tidings to the poor announce;
Proclaim God's year of grace.

When heavenly peace at last goes forth
From Zion's holy height,
O come, Messiah King,
To reign in endless light. Amen.[69]

PSALM 141:1–4, 5, 8–9   **RECEIVE MY PRAYER AS INCENSE TEV**

ANTIPHON Drop down dew, you heavens from
    above, * AND LET THE EARTH BRING FORTH
    A SAVIOR.

I call to you, LORD, help me now!
  Listen to me when I call to you.
Receive my prayer as incense,
  my uplifted hands as an evening sacrifice.

ANTIPHON DROP DOWN DEW, YOU HEAVENS FROM
    ABOVE, AND LET THE EARTH BRING FORTH A
    SAVIOR.

LORD, place a guard at my mouth,
  a sentry at the door of my lips.
Keep me from wanting to do wrong
  and from joining evil people in their wickedness.

ANTIPHON DROP DOWN DEW, YOU HEAVENS FROM
ABOVE, AND LET THE EARTH BRING FORTH A
SAVIOR.

Good people may punish me
  and rebuke me in kindness,
but I will never accept honor from evil people,
  because I am always praying against their evil
    deeds.

ANTIPHON DROP DOWN DEW, YOU HEAVENS FROM
ABOVE, AND LET THE EARTH BRING FORTH A
SAVIOR.

I keep trusting in you, my Sovereign LORD.
  I seek your protection; don't let me die!
Protect me from the traps they have set for me,
  from the snare of those evildoers.

ANTIPHON DROP DOWN DEW, YOU HEAVENS FROM
ABOVE, AND LET THE EARTH BRING FORTH A
SAVIOR.

Glory to the Father, and to the Son,
  and to the Holy Spirit:
as it was in the beginning, is now,
  AND WILL BE FOR EVER. Amen.

ANTIPHON DROP DOWN DEW, YOU HEAVENS FROM
ABOVE, AND LET THE EARTH BRING FORTH A
SAVIOR.

PSALM PRAYER
Let us pray (pause for silent adoration):

Great and merciful God,
in your tender compassion
the dawn from on high
breaks upon us in Jesus
and guides us into the way of peace.
Be pleased to illumine and guard us
at the heart of your holy Church
that we may worship you in spirit and truth
as we rejoice before your holy tabernacles,
now and always and for ever and ever.
~AMEN.

We pray Psalm 85 and/or the Canticle of Isaiah.

PSALM 85 THE AGE OF PEACE AND JUSTICE

ANTIPHON God will speak peace * TO THE PEOPLE.

Lord, you showed favor to your land;
  you restored the fortunes of Jacob.
You forgave the iniquity of your people;
  you pardoned all their sin.
You withdrew all your wrath;
  you turned from your hot anger.

Restore us again, O God of our salvation,
  and put away your indignation toward us!
Will you be angry with us forever?
  Will you prolong your anger to all generations?

Will you not revive us again,
  that your people may rejoice in you?
Show us your steadfast love, O Lord,
  and grant us your salvation.

Let me hear what God the Lord will speak,
  for God will speak peace to the people,
  to the faithful, to those who turn to God
    in their hearts.
Surely salvation is at hand,
  for those who fear the Lord,
  that glory may dwell in our land.

Steadfast love and faithfulness will meet;
  righteousness and peace will kiss each other.
Faithfulness will spring up from the ground,
  and righteousness will look down from the sky.

The Lord will give what is good,
  and our land will yield its increase.
Righteousness will go before the Lord,
  and make a path for God's footsteps.

ANTIPHON GOD WILL SPEAK PEACE TO THE PEOPLE.

PSALM PRAYER

Let us pray (pause for silent adoration):

God of our salvation,
in the time of Jesus, your anointed Son,
righteousness and peace shall kiss each other
as you bring to completion all the promises
made to your holy prophets.
Pardon all our sins,
and speak peace to the people,
who turn to you in the tabernacle.
Blest be Jesus, now and for ever.
~AMEN.

ANTIPHON On that day * THE ROOT OF JESSE SHALL
STAND AS A SIGNAL TO THE PEOPLES.

A shoot shall sprout from the stump of Jesse,
  and from his roots a bud shall blossom.
The spirit of the LORD shall rest upon him,
  a spirit of wisdom and understanding,
A spirit of counsel and of strength,
  a spirit of knowledge and of fear of the Lord,
  and his delight shall be the fear of the Lord.

Not by appearance shall he judge,
  nor by hearsay shall he decide,
But he shall judge the poor with justice,
  and shall decide aright for the land's afflicted.

He shall strike the ruthless with the rod of his
      mouth,
  and with the breath of his lips he shall slay the
      wicked.
Justice shall be the band around his waist,
  and faithfulness a belt upon his hips.

Then the wolf shall be a guest of the lamb,
  and the leopard shall lie down with the kid;
the calf and the young lion shall browse together,
  with a little child to guide them.

The cow and the bear shall be neighbors,
  together their young shall rest;
  the lion shall eat hay like the ox.

The baby shall play by the cobra's den
   and the child lay his hand on the adder's lair.

There shall be no harm or ruin on all my holy
      mountain;
   for the earth shall be filled with knowledge of the
      LORD,
         as waters cover the sea.

ANTIPHON ON THAT DAY THE ROOT OF JESSE SHALL
      STAND AS A SIGNAL TO THE PEOPLES.

PRAYER

Let us pray (pause for silent adoration):

May Jesus, the Messiah and Lord,
the descendant of Jesse and David,
pour out his Spirit on humankind
for the welfare of all nations and peoples
that stand in awe of his Real Presence
   in our tabernacles.
His reign is a reign for all ages.
~AMEN.

READING FOR
ADVENT   FREEDOM   ISAIAH 61:1–2

The spirit of the LORD God is upon me, because
the LORD has anointed me; he has sent me to
bring good news to the oppressed, to bind up the
brokenhearted, to proclaim liberty to the captives,
and release to the prisoners; to proclaim the year
of the LORD's favor.

Or this reading:

JEREMIAH

READING   **A MESSIANIC ORACLE**   **23:5–6**

The days are surely coming, says the LORD, when I will raise up for David a righteous Branch, and he shall reign as king and deal wisely, and shall exercise justice and righteousness in the land. In his days Judah shall be saved and Israel shall live in safety. And this is the name by which he shall be called: "The LORD is our righteousness."

Pause for Silent Adoration

RESPONSE

Hail, Mary, full of grace, alleluia!
~THE LORD IS WITH YOU, ALLELUIA!

THE CANTICLE OF THE VIRGIN MARY   LUKE 1:46–55

ANTIPHON   The Virgin will give birth to a Son *
AND THEY WILL CALL HIM EMMANUEL,
      GOD-IS-WITH-US.

My soul † proclaims the greatness of the Lord,
my spirit rejoices in God my Savior,
for you, Lord, have looked with favor on your
      lowly servant.

From this day all generations will call me blessed:
      you, the Almighty, have done great things for
      me
and holy is your name.

You have mercy on those who fear you,
from generation to generation.

You have shown strength with your arm
and scattered the proud in their conceit,
casting down the mighty from their thrones
and lifting up the lowly.
You have filled the hungry with good things
and sent the rich away empty.

You have come to the aid of your servant Israel,
to remember the promise of mercy,
the promise made to our forebears,
to Abraham and his children for ever.

To the Ruler of the ages,
immortal, invisible, the only wise God,
be honor and glory, through Jesus Christ,
for ever and ever. Amen.

ANTIPHON THE VIRGIN WILL GIVE BIRTH TO A SON
AND THEY WILL CALL HIM EMMANUEL,
GOD-IS-WITH-US.

Act of Dedication to Christ Incarnate

The leader recites each section of this prayer and all
respond with the refrain.

Blessed be Jesus in the Most Holy Sacrament of
the Altar!
You came for us in Mary's womb, the incarnate
Son of God,

and you will come again in glory to judge the
world.

ALL: ~Praise to you, Lord Christ.

Because you are our Lord and Savior
we attach ourselves more firmly to your Sacred
Presence
in the Most Holy Sacrament of the Altar
and dedicate ourselves to your service.

ALL: ~Praise to you, Lord Christ.

Have mercy on your one, holy, catholic, and
apostolic Church
and make its members faithful to their baptismal
promises.
You invite us to sit at your right hand with all the
saints in glory.

ALL: ~Praise to you, Lord Christ.

Draw all Christian believers to you in the Blessed
Sacrament
and all those who do not yet believe in your
Presence.
Forgive all lukewarm souls and attract them by
your love.

ALL: ~Praise to you, Lord Christ.

Make the earth resound from pole to pole with a
single cry:
Praise to the Divine Heart that gained our
salvation;

A Holy Hour for the Season of Advent **141**

glory and honor be his for ever and ever. Amen.

ALL: ~PRAISE TO YOU, LORD CHRIST.

Advent Litany

O Wisdom, breath of the Most High,
   pervading and controlling all creation
   with strength and tenderness:
~COME, AND TEACH US THE WAY OF TRUTH.

O Lord of lords and Leader of the house of Israel,
   who appeared to Moses in the burning bush
   and gave him the Law on Sinai:
~COME, AND SAVE US BY YOUR MIGHTY ARM.

O Flower of Jesse's stock, a signal to the nations;
   kings stand mute before you
   and all peoples pay you homage:
~COME, DELIVER US, DELAY NO LONGER.

O Key of David and Ruler of the house of Israel,
   opening the gate of heaven to all believers:
~COME, AND SET YOUR CAPTIVE PEOPLE FREE.

O radiant Dawn, splendor of eternal light
   and sun of righteousness:
~COME, AND SHINE ON THOSE WHO SIT IN
      DARKNESS AND THE SHADOW OF DEATH.

O Ruler of all the nations, so long-desired,
   the cornerstone of the human household:
~COME AND SAVE THOSE WHOM YOU HAVE
      FASHIONED FROM THE DUST.

O Emmanuel, our Ruler and our lawgiver,
   the awaited of the nations and their Savior:
~Come, Lord God, and set us free.[70]

Pause for our special intentions.

THE LORD'S PRAYER
Lord, have mercy.
~Christ, have mercy. Lord, have mercy.

Our Father in heaven, (all in unison) . . .

CLOSING PRAYERS
Father in heaven,
our hearts desire the warmth of your love
and our minds are searching for the light of your
      Word.
Increase our longing for Christ our Savior
and give us the strength to grow in your love,
that the day of his coming
may find us rejoicing in his presence
and welcoming the light of his truth.
We ask this in the name of Jesus the Lord.
~Amen.[71]

Or this prayer:

Father, all-powerful God,
your eternal Word took flesh on our earth
when the Virgin Mary placed her life
at the service of your plan.
Lift our minds in watchful hope

to hear the voice which announces his glory
and open our minds to receive the Spirit
who prepares us for his coming.
We ask this through Christ our Lord.
~AMEN.[72]

Blessed be Jesus in the Most Holy Sacrament of
the Altar,
~NOW AND ALWAYS AND FOR EVER AND EVER!
AMEN.

May the God of peace ✝ make us perfect and holy
and keep us safe and blameless, spirit and body,
for the coming of our Lord Jesus Christ.
~AMEN.

A *public* Holy Hour always concludes with
Benediction of the Blessed Sacrament. See pages
104–106.

Since a key link between Advent and Christmas is
Mary of Nazareth, let us look at Mary on the eve of
the incarnation and the birth of Jesus in the stable of
Bethlehem as was envisioned by the great English
mystic, Blessed Julian of Norwich.

The Annunciation

*God brought our Lady to my understanding.
I saw her spiritually in her bodily likeness, a
simple, humble maiden, young in years, of the
stature which she had when she conceived.
Also God showed me part of the wisdom and
truth of her soul, and in this I understood the reverent contemplation with which she beheld her*

God, marveling with great reverence that he was willing to be born of her who was a simple creature created by him. And this wisdom and truth, this knowledge of her Creator's greatness and of her created littleness, made her say meekly to the angel Gabriel: Behold me here, God's handmaiden. In this sight I saw truly that she is greater, more worthy and more fulfilled, than everything else that God has created and which is inferior to her. Above her is no created thing, except the blessed humanity of Christ.

Blessed Julian of Norwich (ca. 1342–1423)[73]

A Holy Hour for Christmastide

Bethlehem, the House of Bread, the House of David, is the birthplace of our Lord Jesus, the Word of God made flesh who came to dwell among us. Just as Jesus dwelt for nine months in his mother's womb so Jesus lives on in the Blessed Sacrament in our tabernacles. Christmas is a daily experience for those who come to adore the sacramental Presence that cannot wane or waver. Jesus stays with us until the end of the age.

Emmanuel, God-is-with-us, is the name of the Messiah, God's Anointed, who is revealed in the mysteries of the Christmas cycle. Mary was the first to welcome him by faith and against all appearances: "Blessed is she who believed" (Luke 2:45). Joseph, too, embraced without hesitation God's puzzling ways in pure faith and took Mary, his espoused and pregnant wife, to be his bride (Matthew 1:24). Even in his mother's womb, John the Baptist "leaped for joy" in the presence of the Messiah hidden in Mary's womb (Luke 1:44). At his actual birth at Bethlehem, a handful of ignorant shepherds, a few wise men following a star, and, a little later, some old folks in the Temple, came to recognize and acknowledge the Light of the world. But there is more than joy to the mystery of Christmas. Remember Herod and the massacre of the Holy Innocents of Bethlehem.

Light and peace ✝ in Jesus Christ our Lord.
~THANKS BE TO GOD.
You are the bright and the morning Star,
~O CHRIST OUR LORD.

PSALM 117   UNIVERSAL PRAISE

ANTIPHON Praise to you, * LORD JESUS CHRIST!

Praise the Lord, all nations!
  Extol the Lord, all peoples!
~PRAISE TO YOU, LORD JESUS CHRIST!

Great is the Lord's steadfast love for us!
  The faithfulness of the Lord endures forever!
~PRAISE TO YOU, LORD JESUS CHRIST!

Glory to the Father, and to the Son,
  and to the Holy Spirit:
~PRAISE TO YOU, LORD JESUS CHRIST!

As it was in the beginning, is now,
  and will be for ever. Amen.
~PRAISE TO YOU, LORD JESUS CHRIST!

PSALM PRAYER

Let us pray *(pause for silent adoration):*

Gracious Lord and Savior,
you selected servants to reveal your mysteries:
From the angels, Gabriel,
from mortals, the Virgin Mary,
from the heavens, a star,
from the rivers, the Jordan,
in order to wash away the sins
of the whole world.
Glory to you, Lord Christ, glory to you!
~AMEN[74]

HYMN

To us a Child of hope is born,
To us a Son is given;
Him shall the tribes of earth obey,
Him all the hosts of heaven.

His name shall be the Prince of Peace,
For evermore adored,
The Wonderful, the Counselor,
The great and mighty Lord.

His power increasing still shall spread,
His reign no end shall know;
Justice shall guard his throne above
And peace abound below. Amen.[75]

We pray Psalm 2 and/or A Canticle of Isaiah.

PSALM 2   GOD PROCLAIMS THE ANOINTED SON

ANTIPHON You are my Son, * TODAY I HAVE
    BEGOTTEN YOU, ALLELUIA!

Why do the nations conspire
  and the people plot in vain?
The kings of the earth rise up,
  and the rulers take counsel together
  against God and God's anointed, saying,
"Let us burst their bonds,
  and cast their cords from us."

The One who sits in the heavens laughs,
  and holds them in derision.

Then God will speak to them in anger,
  and terrify them in fury, saying,
"I have set my king on Zion, my holy hill."

I will tell the decree of the Lord
  who said to me: "You are my son,
  today I have begotten you.
Ask of me, and I will make the nations your heritage,
  and the ends of the earth your possession.
You shall break them with a rod of iron,
  and dash them in pieces like a potter's vessel."

Now, therefore, O kings, be wise;
  be warned, O rulers of the earth.
Serve the Lord with fear and trembling;
  humble yourselves before the Lord
lest God be angry, and you perish in the way;
  for God's wrath is quickly kindled.
Blessed are all who take refuge in the Lord.

ANTIPHON YOU ARE MY SON, TODAY I HAVE
  BEGOTTEN YOU, ALLELUIA!

PSALM PRAYER

Let us pray (pause for silent adoration):

Lord Jesus, Anointed Son of God,
Daystar from on high and Prince of peace,
fill the world with your splendor,
shelter us from tyrants and exploiters,
and show the nations the light of your truth.
Your reign is a reign for all ages.
~AMEN.

A Canticle of Isaiah the Prophet   **Isaiah 9:2–6**

Antiphon The zeal of the Lord of hosts * WILL DO
     THIS!

The people who walked in darkness
  have seen a great light;
those who lived in a land of deep darkness—
  on them light has shined.

You have multiplied the nation,
  you have increased its joy;
they rejoice before you
  as with joy at the harvest,
  as people exult when dividing plunder.

For a child has been born for us,
  a son given to us;
authority rests upon his shoulders;
  and he is named
Wonderful Counselor, Mighty God,
  Everlasting Father, Prince of Peace.

His authority shall grow continually,
  and there shall be endless peace
for the throne of David and his kingdom.
He will establish and uphold it
  with justice and righteousness
  from this time onward and forevermore.

Antiphon THE ZEAL OF THE LORD OF HOSTS WILL
     DO THIS!

PRAYER

Let us pray (pause for silent adoration):

Lord Jesus Christ,
you are the light and life of the world,
and have increased the joy of the human race.
By your sacramental presence among us,
shine on the darkness of our misery
and illuminate our understanding
of the good news preached to us.
You endure through all the ages of ages.
~AMEN.

READINGS FOR CHRISTMASTIDE

THE WORD
DECEMBER 25–31   OF LIFE   1 JOHN 1:1–3 TEV

Brothers and sisters, we write to you about the
Word of life, which has existed from the very
beginning. We have heard it, and we have seen it
with our own eyes; yes, we have seen it, and our
hands have touched it. When this life became
visible, we saw it; so we speak of it and tell you
about the eternal life which was with the Father
and was made known to us. What we have seen
and heard we announce to you also, so that you
will join with us in the fellowship that we have
with the Father and with his Son Jesus Christ.

JANUARY 1–5:   **THE WOMAN**   **GALATIANS 4:4–7**

When the fullness of time had come, God sent his Son, born of a woman, under the law, in order to redeem those who were under the law, so that we might receive adoption as children. And because you are children, God has sent the Spirit of his Son into our hearts, crying, "Abba! Father!" So you are no longer a slave but a child, and if a child then also an heir, through God.

In Canada and the United States the Epiphany is celebrated on the first Sunday after New Year's Day, and the feast of the Baptism of the Lord on the second Sunday.

JANUARY 6–13:   **EPIPHANY/ BAPTISM**   **ISAIAH 62:1–3**

For Zion's sake I will not keep silent, and for Jerusalem's sake I will not rest, until her vindication shines out like the dawn, and her salvation like a burning torch. The nations shall see your vindication, and all the kings your glory; and you shall be called by a new name that the mouth of the LORD will give. You shall be a crown of beauty in the hand of the LORD, and a royal diadem in the hand of your God.

Pause for Silent Adoration.

RESPONSE

The Word became flesh, alleluia!

~AND LIVED AMONG US, ALLELUIA!

The Canticle of the Word   John 1:1–5, 10–12, 14

Antiphons

Dec. 25–31: Glory to God in the highest, alleluia! *
and peace to God's people on earth,
    alleluia!

Jan. 1–5: O wondrous exchange! *
The Creator of the human race,
having assumed our human nature,
was born of the Virgin Mary
and enriched us with his divinity, alleluia!

Jan. 6 and 13: The Church is joined to her
    heavenly spouse: * Christ washes away
    her sins in the Jordan,
the Magi hurry with gifts to the royal
    wedding,
the guests are made glad by water made
    wine, alleluia!

We make a full sign of the cross to begin the gospel canticle.

In the beginning † was the Word,
and the Word was with God,
and the Word was God.
He was in the beginning with God.
All things came into being through him
and without him not one thing came into being.

What has come into being in him was life,
and the life was the light of all people.

The light shines in the darkness,
and the darkness did not overcome it.

He was in the world,
and the world came into being through him;
yet the world did not know him.

He came to what was his own,
and his own people did not accept him.
But to all who received him,
who believed in his name,
he gave power to become children of God.

And the Word became flesh
and lived among us,
and we have seen his glory,
the glory of the Father's only Son,
full of grace and truth.

To the Ruler of the ages, immortal, invisible,
    the only wise God,
be honor and glory, through Jesus Christ,
    for ever and ever. Amen.

The proper antiphon is repeated.

Act of Dedication to Jesus of Bethlehem

The leader recites each section of this prayer and all
respond with the refrain.

Gracious Lord and Redeemer of the world,
born of the Virgin Mary in the cave of Bethlehem,

we renew our commitment to you
in the Blessed Sacrament of the Altar.

ALL: ~PRAISE TO THE BABE OF BETHLEHEM!

Lord Jesus, true God and true Man,
renew the mystery of the incarnation in our hearts
and establish all the sacred truths of our religion
more firmly in our minds and hearts.

ALL: ~PRAISE TO THE BABE OF BETHLEHEM!

Jesus, born in poverty and insecurity,
draw us to the spiritual and corporal works of mercy
that we may be the true disciples of your example.

ALL: ~PRAISE TO THE BABE OF BETHLEHEM!

Jesus of Bethlehem and Nazareth,
hymned by adoring angels, revered by shepherds,
worshipped by wise men from the East,
open the mysteries of the Holy Eucharist
to our hearts and minds.

ALL: ~PRAISE TO THE BABE OF BETHLEHEM!

Make the earth resound from pole to pole with a
    single cry:
Praise to the Divine Heart that gained our
    salvation;
glory and honor be his for ever and ever. Amen.

ALL: ~PRAISE TO THE BABE OF BETHLEHEM!

Christmas Litany

By the great mysteries of the Word made flesh
for us, we pray:

~LORD, HAVE MERCY.

By the wondrous birth in time of the eternal Son
of God, we pray:

~LORD, HAVE MERCY.

By the humble nativity of the King of glory
in Bethlehem of Judea, we pray:

~LORD, HAVE MERCY.

By the radiant manifestation of the Babe of
Bethlehem to the shepherds and the magi,
we pray:

~LORD, HAVE MERCY.

By the meeting of the Infant Jesus with old Simeon
and Anna in the Temple, we pray:

~LORD HAVE MERCY.

By the revealing of the Holy Trinity in the baptism
of God's beloved Son in the Jordan, we pray:

~LORD, HAVE MERCY.

By the lowly submission of the Maker of the world
to Mary and Joseph of Nazareth, we pray:

~LORD, HAVE MERCY.

By the first of his signs at Cana of Galilee, we pray:

~LORD, HAVE MERCY.

Pause for our special intentions.

In the communion of the great Mother of God,
    Mary most holy,
St. Joseph, her spouse, and of all the saints in
    glory,
let us commend ourselves, one another,
and our whole life to Christ our Lord.
~To you, O Lord.

THE LORD'S PRAYER
Lord, have mercy.
~Christ, have mercy. Lord, have mercy.

Our Father in heaven, (all in unison) . . .

CLOSING PRAYERS
December 25–31:
Abba, dear Father,
each year you make us glad
by the birth of your only Son Jesus Christ.
May we who joyfully receive him
as our Redeemer,
welcome him with confidence
when he comes to be our Judge;
he lives and reigns with you,
in the unity of the Holy Spirit,
one God, now and for ever.
~Amen.[76]

January 1–5:
God our Father,
may we always profit by the prayers
of the Virgin Mother Mary,
for you bring us life and salvation
through Jesus Christ her Son
who lives and reigns with you and the Holy Spirit,
one God, for ever and ever.[77]
~AMEN.

In Canada and the United States the Epiphany is
celebrated on the first Sunday after New Year's Day,
and the feast of the Baptism of the Lord on the
second Sunday.

Epiphany:
Father of light, unchanging God,
you reveal to those of faith
the resplendent fact of the Word made flesh.
Your light is strong, your love is near;
draw us beyond the limits which this world
        imposes
to the life where the Spirit makes all life complete.
We ask this through Christ our Lord.
~AMEN.[78]

Baptism:
Heavenly Father,
glory of all who believe in you,
you fill the world with your splendor
and reveal to those of good will

the light of your truth,
through Jesus Christ our Lord,
who lives and reigns with you,
in the unity of the Holy Spirit,
one God for ever and ever.
~Amen.[79]

Blessed be Jesus in the Most Holy Sacrament of
the Altar,
~Now and always and for ever and ever.
Amen.

May the Lord Christ, incarnate in our human
nature, ✝ bless us and keep us. Amen.

A *public* Holy Hour concludes with Benediction of
the Blessed Sacrament. See pages 104–106.

A Holy Hour for Lent

The forty days of Lent were originally established in the fourth century as the final stage for those who were to be baptized during the Easter Vigil. This season still carries that emphasis, both for those about to be initiated and for those who are going to renew their baptismal vows at Easter.

Inspired by the example and fervor of such new Christians, the baptized want to renew their commitment to Christ and to promise again to live up to their baptismal promises. New Christians and old Christians meet together in faith during Lent and, above all, during the Easter Vigil. The former are immersed in water and the Holy Spirit and made new creatures in Christ while the latter renew and reaffirm their baptism through the sacrament of Reconciliation and the public renewal of their baptismal vows. The climax is the celebration of the Easter Eucharist and the union of all at the altar in Holy Communion.

Traditionally, Lent calls for three observances: prayer, fasting and almsgiving: *prayer* to fix the mind on Christ and the Gospel message; *fasting* to help the body share in the sufferings of Jesus and of the poor and to set aside money for *almsgiving* to those in need. Almsgiving includes gifts of time, money, and commitment to the corporal and spiritual works of mercy.

The *corporal works of mercy* are feed the hungry, give drink to the thirsty, clothe the naked, shelter the homeless, visit the sick, visit prisoners, and bury the dead.

The *spiritual works of mercy* are counsel the doubtful, instruct the ignorant, admonish sinners, comfort the afflicted, forgive offenses, bear wrongs patiently, and pray for the living and the dead.

The reign of God ✝ is near at hand;
~COME, LET US ADORE HIM.
How precious, O God, is your constant love.
~WE FIND PROTECTION IN THE SHADOW OF YOUR
WINGS.

PSALM 95:1–7 AN INVITATION TO PRAISE AND PRAYER

ANTIPHON Come, let us worship the Lord *
WHO CALLS US TO CHANGE OUR HEARTS AND
MINDS.

O come, let us sing to the Lord;
  let us make a joyful noise
  to the rock of our salvation!
Let us come into God's presence
  with thanksgiving;
  let us make a joyful noise with songs of praise!

ANTIPHON COME, LET US WORSHIP THE LORD
WHO CALLS US TO CHANGE OUR HEARTS AND
MINDS.

For the Lord is a great God,
  and a great Ruler above all gods,
in whose hands are the depths of the earth
  and also the heights of the mountains.
The sea belongs to God who made it,
  and the dry land, because God formed it.

ANTIPHON COME, LET US WORSHIP THE LORD
WHO CALLS US TO CHANGE OUR HEARTS AND
MINDS.

O come, let us worship and bow down,
  let us kneel before the Lord, our Maker!
For the Lord is our God,
  we are the people of God's pasture,
  the sheep of God's hand.
Hear the voice of the Lord today!

ANTIPHON COME, LET US WORSHIP THE LORD
WHO CALLS US TO CHANGE OUR HEARTS AND
    MINDS.

Glory to the Father, and to the Son,
  and to the Holy Spirit:
as it was in the beginning, is now,
  and will be for ever. Amen.

ANTIPHON COME, LET US WORSHIP THE LORD
WHO CALLS US TO CHANGE OUR HEARTS AND
    MINDS.

PSALM PRAYER
Let us pray (pause for silent adoration):

By Christ our teacher, O God,
you invite us to repentance—
to a change of mind and heart.
By the grace and gift of our Savior,
transform our life
and submit us to your holy will
that we may be your faithful creatures
in thought, word, and deed;
through the same Christ our Lord.
~AMEN.

HYMN

Now let us all with one accord,
In company with ages past,
Keep vigil with our heavenly Lord
In his temptation and his fast.

The covenant so long revealed
To those of faith in former time,
Christ by his own example sealed,
The Lord of love, in love sublime.

Your love, O Lord, our sinful race
Has not returned, but falsified;
Author of mercy turn your face
And grant repentance for our pride.

Therefore we pray you, Lord, forgive;
So when our wand'rings here shall cease,
We may with you for ever live,
In love and unity and peace. Amen.[80]

We pray Psalm 51 and/or the Canticle of Manasseh.

PSALM 51   A PLEA FOR FORGIVENESS NAB

ANTIPHON If we die with the Lord, *
WE SHALL LIVE WITH THE LORD.
Have mercy on me, God, in your goodness;
  in your abundant compassion blot out my
        offense.
Wash away all my guilt;
  from my sin cleanse me.
For I know my offense;
  my sin is always before me.

Against you alone have I sinned;
I have done such evil in your sight
that you are just in your sentence,
blameless when you condemn.
True I was born guilty,
  a sinner, even as my mother conceived me.

Still you insist on sincerity of heart;
  in my inmost being teach me wisdom.
Cleanse me with hyssop, that I may be pure;
  wash me, make me whiter than snow.
Let me hear sounds of joy and gladness;
  let the bones you have crushed rejoice.

Turn away your face from my sins;
  blot out all my guilt.
A clean heart create for me, God;
  renew in me a steadfast spirit.

Do not drive me away from your presence,
  nor take from me your holy spirit.
Restore my joy in your salvation;
  sustain in me a willing spirit.
I will teach the wicked your ways,
  that sinners may return to you.

Rescue me from death, God, my saving God,
  that my tongue may praise your healing power.
Lord, open my lips;
  my mouth will proclaim your praise.

For you do not desire sacrifice;
  a burnt offering you would not accept.

My sacrifice, God, is a broken spirit;
  do not spurn a broken, humbled heart.

ANTIPHON IF WE DIE WITH THE LORD,
WE SHALL LIVE WITH THE LORD.

PSALM PRAYER
Let us pray (pause for silent adoration):

Abbà, gracious Father,
when King David repented before you
at the warnings of Nathan the prophet,
you poured out on him
the healing medicine of your forgiveness.
By following David's example,
give us a sincere and humble heart,
and renew us in the Holy Spirit,
that we may adore you in the Blessed Sacrament
in season and out of season,
to the honor and glory of Christ our Lord.
~AMEN.

The Canticle of Manasseh 1, 2, 4, 6–7, 11–12, 13–15

ANTIPHON O Lord, * YOU ARE THE GOD OF THOSE
        WHO REPENT.

O Lord almighty, God of our ancestors,
you made heaven and earth with all their order.
All things shudder and tremble before your power.

Yet immeasurable and unsearchable
is your promised mercy,

for you are the Lord Most High,
of great compassion, long-suffering,
    and very merciful,
and you relent at human suffering.

And now I bend the knee of my heart,
imploring you for your kindness.
I have sinned, O Lord, I have sinned,
and I acknowledge my transgressions.

For you, O Lord, are the God of those who repent,
and in me you will manifest your goodness;
for, unworthy as I am, you will save me
according to your great mercy.

I will praise you continually
all the days of my life.
For all the hosts of heaven sing your praise,
and yours is the glory for ever. Amen.

ANTIPHON O LORD, YOU ARE THE GOD OF THOSE
    WHO REPENT.

PRAYER

Let us pray (pause for silent adoration):

Merciful and compassionate Father,
our first beginning and our last end,
guard and guide our restless hearts:
Inspire us to love you completely
and to serve you with generosity;
for the sake of Jesus Christ our Lord.
~AMEN.

READING   **DRY BONES**   **EZEKIEL 37:4–6** TEV

The LORD said to Ezekiel: "Prophesy to the bones.
Tell these dry bones to listen to the word of the
LORD. Tell them that I, the Sovereign LORD, am
saying to them: I am going to put breath into you
and bring you back to life. I will give you sinews
and muscles, and cover you with skin. I will put
breath into you and bring you back to life. Then
you will know that I am the Lord."

Pause for Silent Adoration.

RESPONSE

I will put my breath in you
~AND BRING YOU BACK TO LIFE.

Or, this reading:

            LUKE 6:20–26
READING   **THE BEATITUDES**   NAB

Blessed are you who are poor,
     for the kingdom of God is yours.
Blessed are you who are now hungry,
     for you will be satisfied.
Blessed are you who are now weeping,
     for you will laugh.
Blessed are you when people hate you,
   and when they exclude and insult you,
   and denounce your name as evil
   on account of the Son of Man.

Rejoice and leap for joy on that day.
　　Behold, your reward will be great in heaven.
　　For their ancestors treated the prophets
　　in the same way.

But woe to you who are rich;
　　for you have received your consolation.
But woe to you who are filled now,
　　for you will be hungry.
Woe to you who laugh now,
　　for you will grieve and weep.
Woe to you when all speak well of you,
　　for their ancestors treated the false prophets
　　in this way.

Pause for Silent Adoration.

RESPONSE

The Lord does not seek the death of sinners,
~BUT RATHER THAT THEY BE CONVERTED AND
　　LIVE.

THE CANTICLE OF THE	REVELATION
LAMB OF GOD	4:11; 5:9–10, 12

ANTIPHON The blood of Jesus, God's Son, *
CLEANSES US FROM ALL SIN.

You are worthy, our Lord and God,
　to receive glory and honor and power,
for you created all things,
　　and by your will they existed and were created.

You are worthy, O Christ,
  to take the scroll and to open its seals,
for you were slaughtered
  and by your blood you ransomed for God
saints from every tribe and language and people
  and nation;
you have made them a kingdom and priests
  serving our God,
  and they will reign on earth.

Worthy is the Lamb that was slain
to receive power and wealth and wisdom and might
and honor and glory and blessing!

ANTIPHON THE BLOOD OF JESUS, GOD'S SON,
CLEANSES US FROM ALL SIN.

An Act of Dedication to Christ

The leader recites each section of this prayer and all
respond with the refrain.

Lord Jesus Christ, Redeemer of the world,
you were lifted up on the cross
so that everyone who believes in you
might have eternal life.

ALL: ~PRAISE TO YOU, LORD JESUS CHRIST.

By the power of your wisdom and might,
draw everyone who believes in you
and everyone who does not believe in you
working in the seven sacraments of holy Church.

ALL: ~PRAISE TO YOU, LORD JESUS CHRIST.

Draw all nations and peoples to the foot of the
    cross
by the intercession of the Virgin Mary, St. Mary
    Magdalene,
and the beloved disciple, who stood near you as
    you died.

ALL: ~PRAISE TO YOU, LORD JESUS CHRIST.

Make the earth resound from pole to pole with a
    single cry:
Praise to the Divine Heart that gained our
    salvation;
glory and honor be his for ever and ever. ~AMEN.

ALL: ~PRAISE TO YOU, LORD JESUS CHRIST.

THE LORD'S PRAYER

Lord, have mercy.
~CHRIST, HAVE MERCY. LORD, HAVE MERCY.

Our Father in heaven, (all in unison) . . .

LENTEN LITANY

For the peace of Christ in the reign of Christ:
~LORD, HEAR OUR PRAYER.
For true faith, undying hope, and genuine love:
~LORD, HEAR OUR PRAYER.
For those who need our care and assistance:
~LORD, HEAR OUR PRAYER.
For the heavily burdened and afflicted:
~LORD, HEAR OUR PRAYER.

For the mentally handicapped and diseased:
~LORD HEAR OUR PRAYER.
For the friendless and abandoned:
~LORD, HEAR OUR PRAYER.
For our beloved dead who died in the Lord:
~LORD, HEAR OUR PRAYER.

Pause for our Special Intentions.

By the prayers of the great Mother of God,
  Mary most holy, and of all the saints in glory:
~LORD, HEAR OUR PRAYER.

CLOSING PRAYER
Grant us, O gracious God,
in all our ways, your help,
in all our uncertainties, your counsel,
in all our trials and temptations, your protection,
in all our sorrows, your peace.
We ask this through Christ our Lord.
~AMEN.

Or, this prayer:

Lord Jesus Christ,
friend of the human race,
you shed your precious blood for us on the cross
and renew this offering without ceasing
    on our altars.
Remember us in all our needs,
save us from the time of trial,

and deliver us from the evil one.
Your reign is a reign for all ages.
~AMEN.

Blessed be Jesus in the Most Holy Sacrament of
the Altar,

~NOW AND ALWAYS AND FOR EVER AND EVER!
AMEN

May almighty God, Source of all Being,
Eternal Word, and Holy Spirit,
† bless us and keep us.
~AMEN.

A *public* Holy Hour concludes with Benediction of
the Blessed Sacrament. See pages 104–106.

St. Leo the Great warns us to stay on watch against the
lures of Satan during the period of Lent but especially
during Holy Week. Let us be on guard against the Evil
One who prowls about seeking to devour us.

Holy Lent

*Certainly, we need to be on our guard all the
year round against the enemy of our salvation,
never leaving any point exposed to the tempter;
but in this season greater prudence and wari-
ness are called for. Satan is raging against us
with fierce hatred.*

*The reason for this is that these are the days
when the power of his ancient hold over us is
being taken away from him and countless captives are being rescued from his grasp. Men
and women, young and old, boys and girls, are*

*being snatched away from him, born again in
the waters of baptism, which are the womb of
Holy Church. No one is refused on account of
sin, because to be born again and to be put
right with God is not something to be earned;
it is a free gift. To add to Satan's chagrin, he
sees lapsed Christians whom he had previously
deceived now returning to the Lord in contrition,
washed clean by their tears of repentance and
the confession of their sins, reconciled to God
and to the community of God's people.*

*He knows, moreover, that in a few weeks time
it will be Good Friday again, the day of the Lord's
passion, and on that day he will be crushed all
over again by the power of Christ's cross. And
after that will come the Easter Vigil, when all the
members of Christ's body will renew their baptismal vows, renouncing him and all his works
with a single triumphant voice.*

St. Leo the Great († 461)[81]

A Holy Hour for Holy Week

This Holy Hour will be most useful on Holy Thursday evening for the vigil before the altar of repose, from the end of the Lord's Supper until midnight.

O Lord, † open my lips.

~AND MY MOUTH SHALL DECLARE YOUR PRAISE.

Jesus eagerly desired to eat the Passover

~ WITH HIS DISCIPLES BEFORE HE SUFFERED.

Jesus provided us with a living memorial

~OF HIS PASSION AND DEATH.

PSALM 95:1–7   AN INVITATION TO PRAISE AND PRAYER

ANTIPHON Come, let us worship the Lord *
WHO GIVES US THE LIVING BREAD FROM HEAVEN.

O come, let us sing to the Lord;
  let us make a joyful noise
  to the rock of our salvation!
Let us come into God's presence
  with thanksgiving;
  let us make a joyful noise with songs of praise!

ANTIPHON COME, LET US WORSHIP THE LORD
WHO GIVES US THE LIVING BREAD FROM HEAVEN.

For the Lord is a great God,
  and a great Ruler above all gods,
in whose hands are the depths of the earth
  and also the heights of the mountains.
The sea belongs to God who made it,
  and the dry land, because God formed it.

Antiphon Come, let us worship the Lord
who gives us the living bread from heaven.

O come, let us worship and bow down,
  let us kneel before the Lord, our Maker!
For the Lord is our God,
  we are the people of God's pasture,
  the sheep of God's hand.
Hear the voice of the Lord today!

Antiphon Come, let us worship the Lord
who gives us the living bread from heaven.

Glory to the Father, and to the Son,
    and to the Holy Spirit:
as it was in the beginning, is now,
    and will be for ever.
~Amen.

Antiphon Come, let us worship the Lord
who gives us the living bread from heaven.

Psalm Prayer
Let us pray (pause for silent adoration):

Lord Jesus Christ,
you loved us and delivered yourself up for us
as an agreeable and fragrant sacrifice to God.
Rescue us from our former darkness
and teach us to walk as children of the light
in all goodness, justice, and truth.
You live and reign, now and for ever.
~Amen.

Hymn of the Cross

Behold love's heart, bared by a lance,
the Lamb of God, self-sacrificed!
All who are heavy-burdened, come,
take refuge in the wounds of Christ.

For God's compassion even falls
on those who mock him as he dies,
and Christ assures the dying thief
this day he'll enter Paradise.

Christ lifted high upon the cross
draws to himself all Adam's kin:
in self-abasement, tasting death,
he dies that we might live in him. Amen.[82]

A Canticle of the Suffering Servant   Isaiah 53:1–5

Antiphon Jesus was pierced for our offenses, *
CRUSHED FOR OUR SINS.

He grew up before the Lord like a tender plant,
  like a root out of arid ground.
He has no beauty, no majesty to draw our eyes,
  no grace to make us delight in him.

He was despised and rejected,
  a man of sorrows and acquainted with grief.
Like one from whom people hid their faces
  he was despised and we esteemed him not.

Surely he has borne our grief and carried our
    sorrows;
  yet we considered him stricken,
  smitten by God, and afflicted.

He was wounded for our transgressions,
  he was bruised for our iniquities.
The punishment that brought us peace
    was laid upon him,
  and by his wounds we are healed.

To the One seated on the throne and to the Lamb
be blessing and honor and glory and might
for ever and ever!

ANTIPHON JESUS WAS PIERCED FOR OUR OFFENSES,
CRUSHED FOR OUR SINS.

PRAYER
Let us pray (pause for silent adoration):

Be present, be present, Lord Jesus,
as we contemplate your crucified body
hanging on the cross.
By your five precious wounds,
fill us with compassion for your suffering
and with true repentance for our sins
as we await your coming in glory,
O Savior of the world,
living and reigning, now and for ever.
~AMEN.

READING   **AT JERUSALEM**   **LUKE 18:31–33**

Then he took the twelve disciples and said to
them, "See, we are going up to Jerusalem, and
everything that is written about the Son of Man
by the prophets will be accomplished. For he will
be handed over to the Gentiles; and he will be
mocked and insulted and spat upon. After they
have flogged him, they will kill him, and on the
third day he will rise again."

Or,

READING   **CHRIST DIED FOR US**   **ROMANS 5:8–10**

God proves his love for us in that while we were
still sinners Christ died for us. Much more surely
then, now that we have been justified by his blood,
will we be saved through him from the wrath
of God. For if while we were enemies, we were
reconciled to God through the death of his Son,
much more surely, having been reconciled, will we
be saved by his life.

Pause for Silent Adoration

RESPONSE

We adore you, O Christ, and we bless you,

~FOR BY YOUR HOLY CROSS YOU HAVE REDEEMED
    THE WORLD.

A Canticle of
St. Peter the Apostle   Letter 1, 2:21–24 TEV

Antiphon Jesus was pierced for our offenses * AND
        CRUSHED FOR OUR SINS.

Christ himself suffered for us
and left us an example,
so that we might follow
in his footsteps.
He committed no sin
and no one ever heard a lie
come from his lips.

When he was insulted,
he did not answer back with an insult;
when he suffered,
he did not threaten,
but placed his hopes in God,
the righteous Judge.

Christ himself carried our sins
in his body to the cross,
so that we might die to sin
and live for righteousness.
It is by his wounds
that you have been healed.

To the Ruler of the ages, immortal, invisible,
   the only wise God,
be honor and glory through Jesus Christ,
   for ever and ever. Amen.

ANTIPHON JESUS WAS PIERCED FOR OUR OFFENSES, AND CRUSHED FOR OUR SINS.

Act of Dedication to Christ the King

The leader recites each section of this prayer and all respond with the refrain.

Loving Jesus, Redeemer of the world,
we are yours, and yours we wish to be.
To bind ourselves to you even more closely
we kneel before you today
and offer ourselves to your most Sacred Heart.

ALL: ~PRAISE TO YOU, OUR SAVIOR AND OUR KING.

Have mercy on all who have never known you
and on all who reject you and refuse to obey you:
gentle Lord, draw them to yourself.

ALL: ~PRAISE TO YOU, OUR SAVIOR AND OUR KING.

Reign over the faithful who have never left you,
reign over those who have squandered their
inheritance,
the prodigal children who now are starving:
bring them back to their Father's house.

ALL: ~PRAISE TO YOU, OUR SAVIOR AND OUR KING.

Reign over those who are misled by error or
divided by discord.

Hasten the day when we shall be one in faith and
    truth,
one flock with you, the one Shepherd.
Give to your Church freedom and peace,
and to all nations justice and order.

ALL: ~PRAISE TO YOU, OUR SAVIOR AND OUR KING.

Make the earth resound from pole to pole with a
    single cry:
Praise to the Divine Heart that gained our
    salvation;
glory and honor be his for ever and ever. Amen.

ALL: ~PRAISE TO YOU, OUR SAVIOR AND OUR KING.

LITANY OF THE PASSION

Jesus Crucified, you shed your precious blood for us
    as you were scourged at the pillar:
~LORD, FORGIVE US OUR SINS.

Jesus Crucified, you shed your precious blood for us
    as your head was pierced with thorns:
~LORD, FORGIVE US OUR SINS.

Jesus Crucified, you shed your precious blood for us
    as you walked the bitter way of the cross:
~LORD, FORGIVE US OUR SINS.

Jesus Crucified, you shed your precious blood for us
    as cruel nails were driven into your hands and
    feet:
~LORD, FORGIVE US OUR SINS.

Jesus Crucified, you shed your precious blood for us
   as you hung in agony on the cross:
~Lord, forgive us our sins.

Jesus Crucified, you shed your precious blood for us
   when a soldier opened your heart with a spear:
~Lord, forgive us our sins.

Jesus Crucified, you shed your precious blood for us
   when we drink anew from the cup of salvation:
~Lord, forgive us our sins.

We Pray for our Special Intentions

Jesus Crucified, by the tears and prayers
   of your sorrowful Mother standing near the
      cross:
~Lord, forgive us our sins.

THE LORD'S PRAYER
Lord, have mercy.
~Christ, have mercy. Lord, have mercy.

Our Father in heaven, (all in unison) . . .

CLOSING PRAYER
Lord Jesus Christ,
you were fastened with nails to the wood of the
      cross
and raised on high for all to see.
As the sun grew dark and the earth quaked,
you surrendered your spirit to your Father,
descended among the dead,

broke open the gates of death,
and freed those bound in darkness.
As angel choirs rejoiced,
you were raised to life again on the third day,
mastering death by your own death,
and canceling the power of sin.
By these mighty deeds on our behalf,
rescue us from our blindness and tepidity,
inspire us anew by your Holy Spirit,
and lead us into a life of prayer and service
worthy of your awesome sacrifice,
O Savior of the world,
living and reigning, now and for ever.
~Amen.

Blessed be Jesus in the Most Holy Sacrament of
the Altar,
~now and always and for ever and ever!
Amen.

May the Lord bless us and take care of us;
May the Lord be kind and gracious to us;
May the Lord look on us with favor
✝ and give us peace.
~Amen.

A *public* Holy Hour always concludes with
Benediction of the Blessed Sacrament. See pages
104–106.

A Holy Hour for Eastertide

Easter, the Christian Passover, is central to the worship of the church, its theology, and the personal life of its members. The fifty days of Easter, from Easter Sunday to Pentecost, are an extended period of celebration for the newly baptized and for those who welcome them into Christ's fold. The church's permanent task is to make disciples, baptize them in the name of the Holy Trinity, and teach them the will of God revealed in Christ Jesus while we trust firmly in his promise to be with us "always, to the end of the age" (Matthew 28:20), and very especially in the Sacrament of the Altar.

During Eastertide the liturgy relives the luminous appearances of its Risen Lord as they are presented to us in the four Gospels. They are not only "the many convincing proofs" (Acts of the Apostles 1:3) of his glorious resurrection from the dead but also our inspiration and encouragement to a full Christian life.

We are Easter people and Alleluia is our song.

St. Augustine of Hippo Regius (354–430)

Christ † is risen, alleluia!

~HE IS RISEN, INDEED, ALLELUIA!

By his death Christ crushed death, alleluia!

~AND BROUGHT LIFE TO THOSE IN THE GRAVE, ALLELUIA!

PSALM 100   **A CALL TO PRAISE AND PRAYER**

ANTIPHON Come, let us worship the Lord Christ *
WHO HAS RISEN FROM THE DEAD, ALLELUIA!

Make a joyful noise to the Lord, all you lands!
  Serve the Lord with gladness!
  Come into God's presence with singing!

ANTIPHON COME, LET US WORSHIP THE LORD
      CHRIST WHO HAS RISEN FROM THE DEAD,
      ALLELUIA!

Know that the Lord, who made us, is God.
  We are the Lord's;
  we are the people of God,
  the sheep of God's pasture.

ANTIPHON COME, LET US WORSHIP THE LORD
      CHRIST WHO HAS RISEN FROM THE DEAD,
      ALLELUIA!

Enter God's gates with thanksgiving,
  and God's courts with praise!
Give thanks and bless God's name!

ANTIPHON COME, LET US WORSHIP THE LORD
      CHRIST WHO HAS RISEN FROM THE DEAD,
      ALLELUIA!

For the Lord is good;
  God's steadfast love endures for ever,
  God's faithfulness to all generations.

ANTIPHON COME, LET US WORSHIP THE LORD
      CHRIST WHO HAS RISEN FROM THE DEAD,
      ALLELUIA!

Glory to the Father, and to the Son,
  and to the Holy Spirit:
as it was in the beginning, is now,
  and will be for ever. Amen.

ANTIPHON COME, LET US WORSHIP THE LORD
        CHRIST WHO HAS RISEN FROM THE DEAD,
        ALLELUIA!

PSALM PRAYER

Let us pray (pause for silent adoration):

Lord Christ, King of glory,
show us your five indelible wounds
in hands, feet, and side,
and deliver us from every doubt
and distracting influence
that will deter us from serving you
with all our heart and soul and mind,
O Savior of the world,
living and reigning with the Father,
in the unity of the Holy Spirit,
now and for ever.
~AMEN.

EASTER HYMN

At the Lamb's high feast we sing
Praise to our victorious King,
Who has washed us in the tide
Flowing from his piercèd side.

Praise we him whose love divine
Gives the guests his blood for wine,

Give his body for the feast,
Love the victim, love the feast.

Where the paschal blood is poured,
Death's dark angel sheathes his sword;
Israel's hosts triumphant go
Through the wave that drowns the foe.

Christ the Lamb, whose blood was shed,
Paschal victim, paschal bread;
With sincerity and love
Eat we manna from above.

Mighty Victim from the sky,
Powers of hell beneath you lie;
Death is conquered in the fight;
You have brought us life and light.

Vict'ry's banner now you wave
Conqu'ring Satan and the grave;
Angels join his praise to tell—
See o'erthrown the prince of hell.

Easter triumph, Easter joy,
Sin alone can these destroy;
From the death of sin set free,
Souls reborn, O Lord, we'll be.

Hymns of glory, songs of praise,
Father, unto you we raise;
And to you, our Risen King,
With the Spirit, praise we sing.

Ad cenam Agni providi,
St. Nicetas of Remesiana (ca.335–ca.414)[83]

We pray Psalm 118 and/or the Easter Anthem.

**Psalm 118:1, 4, 5–9,
13–17, 22–24, 27, 29**   The Lord's Day nab

Antiphon The stone which the builders rejected,
        alleluia! * has become the cornerstone,
        alleluia!

O give thanks to the Lord who is good;
   whose steadfast love endures for ever!
Let those who fear the Lord say:
   "God's steadfast love endures for ever."

Out of my distress I called on the Lord;
   the Lord answered me and set me in a broad
        place.
With the Lord on my side I do not fear.
   What can mortals do to me?

The Lord is on my side to help me;
   I shall look in triumph on those who hate me.
It is better to take refuge in the Lord
   than to put confidence in mortals.

I was pushed hard, so that I was falling,
   but the Lord helped me.
The Lord is my strength and my power;
   the Lord has become my salvation.

There are joyous songs of victory
   in the tents of the righteous:
   "The right hand of the Lord does valiantly,
   the right hand of the Lord is exalted,
   the right hand of the Lord does valiantly!"

I shall not die, but I shall live,
  and recount the deeds of the Lord.

I thank you that you have answered me
  and have become my salvation.
The stone which the builders rejected
  has become the cornerstone.

This is the Lord's doing;
  it is marvelous in our eyes.
This is the day which the Lord has made;
  let us rejoice and be glad in it.

You are my God, and I will give thanks to you.
  You are my God, I will extol you.
O give thanks to the Lord, who is good;
  for God's steadfast love endures for ever!

ANTIPHON THE STONE WHICH THE BUILDERS
    REJECTED, ALLELUIA! HAS BECOME THE
    CORNERSTONE, ALLELUIA!

PSALM PRAYER

Let us pray (pause for silent adoration):

Lord Jesus Christ,
by your cross and resurrection,
you broke the bonds of death
and brought life to those in the grave.
May your blessed passion
be the joy of the whole world
and your rising from the tomb
ever be our song,

O Savior of the world,
living and reigning with the Father,
in the unity of the Holy Spirit,
one God, for ever and ever.
~Amen.

Easter Anthem (1 Corinthians 5:7–8; Romans 6:9–11; 1 Corinthians 15:20–21)

Antiphon I came forth from the Father and came
into the world; * Again, I am leaving the
world and am going to the Father,
alleluia!

Christ, our paschal lamb, has been sacrificed.
Therefore let us celebrate the festival,
not with the old yeast, the yeast of malice and evil,
but with the unleavened bread of sincerity and
truth, alleluia!

Christ, being raised from the dead, will never die
again;
death no longer has dominion over him.
The death he died, he died to sin, once for all;
but the life he lives, he lives to God.
So you also must consider yourselves dead to sin,
And alive to God in Christ Jesus, alleluia!

Christ has been raised from the dead,
the first fruits of those who have died.
For since death came through a human being,
the resurrection of the dead

came also through a human being;
for as all die in Adam,
so all will be made alive in Christ, alleluia!

Glory to the Father, and to the Son,
  and to the Holy Spirit:
as it was in the beginning, is now,
  and will be for ever.
~AMEN.

ANTIPHON I CAME FORTH FROM THE FATHER
AND CAME INTO THE WORLD; AGAIN, I AM
LEAVING THE WORLD AND AM GOING TO THE
FATHER, ALLELUIA!

PRAYER
Let us pray (pause for silent adoration):

Holy and wonderful God,
you so loved the world
that you sent your only Son
to redeem us all.
As we remember all that he did for us,
the cross, the tomb, the glorious resurrection,
the wonderful ascension into heaven,
and his enthronement at the right hand of the
       Father,
may we offer fitting and grateful praise to you
in the Holy Sacrifice of the Mass,
now and always and for ever and ever.
~AMEN.

A Reading from the Holy Gospel According to St. Mark 16:9–20:

When the Sabbath was over, Mary Magdalene, and Mary the mother of James, and Salome bought spices so that they might go and anoint him. And very early on the first day of the week, when the sun had risen, they went to the tomb. They had been saying to one another, "Who will roll away the stone for us from the entrance to the tomb?" When they looked up, they saw that the stone, which was very large, had already been rolled back. As they entered the tomb, they saw a young man, dressed in a white robe, sitting on the right side; and they were alarmed. But he said to them, "Do not be alarmed; you are looking for Jesus of Nazareth, who was crucified. He has been raised; he is not here. Look, there is the place they laid him. But go, tell his disciples and Peter that he is going ahead of you to Galilee; there you will see him, just as he told you." So they went out and fled from the tomb, for terror and amazement had seized them; and they said nothing to anyone, for they were afraid.

(Ten additional Gospel accounts that may be used during the Easter Season are Mark 16:9–20; Matthew 28:1–10/16–20; Luke 24:1–12/13–35/36–53; John 20:1–10/11–18/19–31/21:1–14.)

Pause for Silent Adoration

RESPONSE

This day was made by the Lord, alleluia, alleluia!
~WE REJOICE AND ARE GLAD, ALLELUIA,
ALLELUIA!

THE CANTICLE OF THE CHURCH

We praise you, O God,
we acclaim you as Lord;
all creation worships you,
the Father everlasting.

To you all angels, all the powers of heaven,
the cherubim and seraphim, sing in endless praise:
  Holy, holy, holy Lord, God of power and might,
  heaven and earth are full of your glory.

The glorious company of apostles praise you.
The noble fellowship of prophets praise you.
The white-robed army of martyrs praise you.

Throughout the world the holy Church acclaims
      you:
  Father, of majesty unbounded,
  your true and only Son, worthy of all praise,
  the Holy Spirit, advocate and guide.

You, Christ, are the king of glory,
the eternal Son of the Father.
When you took our flesh to set us free
you humbly chose the Virgin's womb.

You overcame the sting of death
and opened the kingdom of heaven to all believers.

You are seated at God's right hand in glory.
We believe that you will come to be our judge.

Come, then, Lord and help your people,
bought with the price of your own blood,
and bring us with your saints
to glory everlasting.

St. Nicetas of Remesiana (ca. 335–ca. 414)[84]

Act of Dedication to the Risen Christ

The leader recites each section of this prayer and all respond with the refrain.

Lord Jesus Christ, you have redeemed the whole
    world
by your bitter death and glorious resurrection,
seen and preached by eyewitnesses
for us and for our salvation.

ALL: ~PRAISE TO YOU, OUR RISEN LORD AND
    SAVIOR.

For forty days you fortified your disciples
with sound teaching about the kingdom of God
and led them to touch you and eat with you
in order to convince them of your rising.

ALL: ~PRAISE TO YOU, OUR RISEN LORD AND
    SAVIOR.

Reign in the Church that you established to
    preach,
teach, and baptize the nations of the whole world

and prepare them for your second coming
in glory everlasting.

ALL: ~PRAISE TO YOU, OUR RISEN LORD AND
SAVIOR.

Make the earth resound from pole to pole with a
single cry:
Praise to the Divine Heart that gained our
salvation;
glory and honor be his for ever and ever. ~AMEN.

ALL: ~PRAISE TO YOU, OUR RISEN LORD AND
SAVIOR.

EASTER LITANY

We adore you, Lord Jesus Christ, as you ascend
your bitter cross.
~MAY THIS CROSS DELIVER US FROM THE ANGEL
OF DEATH.

We adore your wounded body hanging on the
cross.
~MAY YOUR WOUNDS BE OUR HEALING.

We adore you dead and buried in noble Joseph's
tomb.
~MAY WE REST IN PEACE WITH YOU.

We adore you as you descend among the dead
to enlighten and deliver them.
~MAY WE RISE TOGETHER WITH ALL OUR HOLY
ANCESTORS.

We adore you rising from the dead on the third
    day.
~FREE US FROM THE BURDEN OF OUR SINS.

We adore you ascending into heaven on the
    fortieth day.
~LIFT UP OUR HEARTS TO HEAVENLY THINGS.

We adore you sitting at the right hand of the
    Father.
~RAISE US TO ETERNAL GLORY WITH YOU AND
    ALL YOUR SAINTS.

We adore you coming in glory to judge the living
    and the dead.
~BE NOT OUR JUDGE BUT OUR SAVIOR.[85]

Pause for special intentions.

THE LORD'S PRAYER
Lord, have mercy.
~CHRIST, HAVE MERCY. LORD, HAVE MERCY.

Our Father in heaven, (all in unison): . . .

CLOSING PRAYER
Lord Jesus Christ,
from the bosom of the Father
you descended into the womb of the Virgin,
from the womb you visited the cradle,
from the cradle you came to the cross,
from the cross to the tomb,
from the tomb you arose in glory

and ascended into heaven:
By this great transit of mercy
—you becoming as we are
and we becoming as you are—
grant us, O Savior of the world,
the fullness of our divine adoption
as sons and daughters of the living God.
You live and reign, now and for ever.
~AMEN.[86]

Let us bless the Lord, alleluia, alleluia!
~THANKS BE TO GOD, ALLELUIA, ALLELUIA!

Blessed be Jesus in the Most Holy Sacrament of
    the Altar,
~NOW AND ALWAYS AND FOR EVER AND EVER!
    AMEN.

May the Father of the risen Christ
    bless us and keep us.
~AMEN.

May the risen Christ himself
    graciously smile upon us.
~AMEN.

May the Holy Spirit sent by the risen Christ
    † grant us peace.
~AMEN.

A *public* Holy Hour always concludes with
Benediction of the Blessed Sacrament. See pages
104–106.

Part 4
Novenas and Triduums of Intercessory Prayer

One of the main historic reasons for exposition and adoration of the Blessed Sacrament was to offer prayers of intercession before it. In times of great public distress, disease, floods, civil disturbances, and lesser personal evils, people often asked for exposition of the Host for days or even for weeks at a time. The general forms of intercession take the shape of litanies, even in processions with the Sacrament carried through the streets. Novenas still fruitfully combine both prayers of petition—often in the form of litanies—with adoration of Jesus in the Blessed Sacrament.

The following forms of intercession may be used for nine days (a novena) or for three days (a triduum) of public or private prayer.

The rubrics (directions) for group celebration of novenas are the same as those for the Holy Hour of the Blessed Sacrament. See pages 111–121.

A Novena in Honor of
the Blessed Sacrament

In the name † of the Father, and of the Son, and
   of the Holy Spirit.
~AMEN.

As often as you eat this bread and drink the cup,
~YOU PROCLAIM THE LORD'S DEATH UNTIL HE
   COMES.

HYMN TO THE BLESSED SACRAMENT

Your body, Jesus, once for us was broken,
Your blood outpoured to heal a broken world.
You rose from death in glory of the Spirit,
Your royal flag victoriously unfurled.

So now these signs of Bread and Wine, retelling
Your dying gift, your living self proclaim.
Until you come in splendor at earth's ending
Your people, Lord, your hidden presence here
   acclaim.[87]

PSALM 116:12–9   A PSALM OF THANKSGIVING

ANTIPHON I will offer to you * THE SACRIFICE OF
   THANKSGIVING, ALLELUIA!

What shall I return to the Lord
   for all God's gifts to me?
I will lift up the cup of salvation
   and call on the name of the Lord,

I will pay my vows to the Lord
  in the presence of all God's people.

Precious in the sight of the Lord
  is the death of the faithful.
O Lord, I am your servant;
  I am your servant, the child of your handmaid.
  You have loosed my bonds.

I will offer to you the sacrifice of thanksgiving
  and call on the name of the Lord.
I will pay my vows to the Lord,
  in the presence of all God's people,
in the courts of the house of the Lord,
  in your midst, O Jerusalem.

ANTIPHON I WILL OFFER TO YOU THE SACRIFICE OF
    THANKSGIVING, ALLELUIA!

PSALM PRAYER
Let us pray (pause for silent adoration):

Lord Jesus Christ,
we worship you living among us
in the sacrament of your body and blood.
May we offer to your Father in heaven
the broken bread of undivided love.
May we offer to our brothers and sisters
a life poured out in loving service of that kingdom
where you live with the Father and the Holy Spirit,
one God, for ever and ever.[88]
  ~AMEN.

From the rising of the sun even to its setting my
name is great among the nations, and in every
place incense is offered to my name, and a pure
offering; for my name is great among the nations,
says the Lord of hosts.

Pause for Silent Adoration

RESPONSE

I am the living bread that came down from
    heaven, alleluia!
~WHOEVER EATS OF THIS BREAD WILL LIVE FOR
    EVER, ALLELUIA!

A LITANY OF THE BLESSED SACRAMENT
(see pages 40–42)

NOVENA PRAYER

Lord Jesus Christ,
as we who worship you
in the Blessed Sacrament of the Altar
may we discover your help in the time of our
    need.
    (We state our needs.)
Just as your presence is everlasting
may your help sustain us in every necessity;
you live and reign with the Father,
in the unity of the Holy Spirit,
one God, forever and ever.
~AMEN.

May the heart of Jesus in the Most Blessed
      Sacrament
be praised, adored, and loved, with grateful
      affection,
at every moment, in all the tabernacles of the
      world,
even unto the end of time.
~AMEN.

A *public* novena often concludes with Benediction
of the Blessed Sacrament. See pages 104–106.

A Novena to the
Five Wounds of Jesus

One of the most impressive scenes in the resurrection Gospels is when "doubting" Thomas puts his fingers into the hands and side of Jesus and reassures himself that the Lord is really risen (John 20:28). Our ancestors in the faith found great devotion to the five wounds of our Savior as they cried out in prayer with Thomas the Apostle, "My Lord and my God!" They saw in the five wounds the indelible signs of God's unfailing love for us in Christ. The stunning wounds of prominent stigmatics like Saint Francis of Assisi (1181–1226) and Padre Pio of Pietrelcina (1887–1968), who bore the same five wounds in their flesh, stir up our devotion to the five wounds and encourage us to call upon God in virtue of those wounds to assist us in all our needs, spiritual and temporal.

In the name of the Father, ✝ and of the Son, and of the Holy Spirit.

~AMEN.

Jesus bore our sins in his body on the cross;

~BY HIS WOUNDS WE HAVE BEEN HEALED.

HYMN

O love, how deep, how broad, how high,
How passing thought and fantasy,
That God, the Son of God should take
Our mortal form for mortals' sake.

For us to evil power betrayed,
Scourged, mocked, in purple robe arrayed,

He bore the shameful cross and death,
For us gave up his dying breath.

For us he rose from death again;
For us he went on high to reign;
For us he sent the Spirit here
To guide, to strengthen, and to cheer.

All glory to our Lord and God
For love so deep, so high, so broad:
The Trinity whom we adore
For ever and for evermore.[89]

PSALM 22:1–8, 14–18   THE PASSION OF CHRIST

ANTIPHON They pierced my hands and my feet *
AND LAID ME IN THE DUST OF DEATH.

My God, my God, why have you forsaken me?
 Why are you so far from helping me,
 from the words of my groaning?
O my God, I cry by day, but you do not answer;
 and by night, but find no rest.

Yet you, the praise of Israel,
 are enthroned in holiness.
In you our forebears trusted;
 they trusted, and you delivered them.
To you they cried, and were saved;
 in you they trusted, and were not disappointed.

But I am a worm, not human;
 scorned by others, and despised by the people.

All who see me mock at me,
they make mouths at me, they wag their heads
and say:

"You committed your cause to the Lord;
let the Lord deliver you.
Let the Lord rescue you,
for the Lord delights in you!"

I am poured out like water,
and all my bones are out of joint;
my heart is like wax,
melted within my breast;
my mouth is dried up like a potsherd,
and my tongue sticks to my jaws;
you lay me in the dust of death.

Indeed, dogs surround me;
a company of evildoers encircles me;
my hands and feet are bound;
I can count all my bones;
they stare and gloat over me;
they divide my garments among them,
and cast lots for my clothing.

ANTIPHON THEY PIERCED MY HANDS AND MY FEET
AND LAID ME IN THE DUST OF DEATH.

PSALM PRAYER
Let us pray (pause for quiet adoration):

Lord Jesus Crucified,
your five priceless wounds

are indelible marks of love made visible.
On the cross of pain,
you begged your Father for help
and he rescued you from death and the grave
and raised you into glory.
Come now to our assistance
in our hour of need
and be our precious Savior,
now and for ever.
~AMEN.

JESUS LIFTED UP
READING   ON THE CROSS   JOHN 3:14–17

Jesus said, "Just as Moses lifted up the serpent in the wilderness, so must the Son of Man be lifted up, that whoever believes in him may have eternal life. For God so loved the world that God gave his only Son, so that everyone who believes in him may not perish but have eternal life. Indeed, God did not send the Son into the world to condemn the world, but in order that the world might be saved through him."

Pause for Silent Adoration

RESPONSE

We adore you, O Christ, and we bless you,
~FOR BY YOUR HOLY CROSS YOU HAVE REDEEMED
   THE WORLD.

LITANY OF THE LIFE-GIVING PASSION

Jesus, our blessed Savior, you embraced the bitter
passion for us and for our salvation:

~LORD, HAVE MERCY.

Friend of the human race, you accepted the cross
and your five gaping wounds for us:

~LORD, HAVE MERCY.

Man of Sorrows, the wicked tore holes in your
hands and feet and laid you in the dust of
death:

~LORD, HAVE MERCY.

Your beauty was marred to give us back the
splendor of God:

~LORD, HAVE MERCY.

By your wounds you vanquished hell and put dark
death to flight:

~LORD, HAVE MERCY.

By your piteous death on the cross we are
delivered from death and decay:

~LORD, HAVE MERCY.

By the prayers of the Mother of Sorrows
and of all the martyrs and saints in glory:

~LORD, HAVE MERCY.

PRAYER TO CHRIST'S WOUNDS

Lord Jesus Christ, Son of the living God,
grant that I may aspire to you,
who are most sweet and most delightful.

Grant that my whole spirit and all my inner being
may unceasingly pant after you who are true
   blessedness.
Most merciful Lord, write your wounds in my
   heart with your precious blood,
that I may read in them your suffering and your
   love alike.
Then may the mindfulness of your wounds
remain with me unceasingly in the recesses of my
   heart,
that sorrow for your sufferings may be aroused
   in me
and the ardor of your love may be enkindled in
   me.
Grant also that all creation may grow worthless in
   my eyes,
and that you alone may impart sweetness to my
   heart.
~Amen.

St. Gertrude the Great (1256–1302)[90]

Novena Prayer

Father of mercies,
as we venerate Jesus' five precious wounds,
you promise us everything we need.
May we share in all the blessings they bring us
and especially (We name our needs).

Be praised and thanked for your loving kindness
to us and to all who worship our blessed Savior in
    his passion,
death and resurrection,
who lives and reigns with you,
in the unity of the Holy Spirit,
now and for ever.
~Amen.

By his holy and glorious wounds
may Christ Jesus † protect us and keep us.
~Amen.

A *public* novena often concludes with Benediction
of the Blessed Sacrament. See pages 104–106.

A Novena to the
Sacred Heart of Jesus

From the time the risen Jesus encouraged "doubting" Thomas to put his fingers into his wounds (John 20:28), Christians have been devoted to the five wounds and especially to the wound in his sacred heart that poured out blood and water for our salvation (John 19:34). Saints and mystics down through the ages have found in the heart of Jesus the supreme symbol of his love for us both collectively and individually.

Blood and Water

Access is possible: Christ is the door. It was opened for you when his side was opened by the lance. Remember what flowed out from his side: choose where you want to enter Christ. From the side of Christ as he hung dying on the Cross there flowed out blood and water, when it was pieced by a lance. Your purification is in that water, your redemption is in that blood.

Saint Augustine of Hippo Regius (354–430)[91]

In the name of the Father, † and of the Son, and of the Holy Spirit.

~AMEN.

The blood of Jesus shall be a sign for you
~ON THE HOUSES WHERE YOU LIVE.

HYMN
All you who seek a comfort sure
In trouble and distress,

Whatever sorrow burdens you,
Whatever griefs oppress:

When Jesus gave himself for us
And died upon the tree,
His heart was pierced for love of us;
He died to set us free.

Now hear him as he speaks to us
Those words for ever blest:
"All you who labor, come to me,
And I will give you rest."

O Heart adored by saints on high,
And hope of sinners here,
We place our every trust in you
And lift to you our prayer.[92]

PSALM 33:1–2, 5–6, 9–12   GOD'S GREAT GOODNESS

ANTIPHON The thoughts of God's heart *
STAND TO ALL GENERATIONS.

Rejoice in the Lord, O you righteous!
  Delight in praise, O you upright!
Praise the Lord with the lyre,
  make melody to the Lord with the harp of ten
      strings!

The Lord loves justice and righteousness;
  the earth is full of the steadfast love of the Lord.
By the word of the Lord the heavens were made,
  and all their host by the breath of God's mouth.

For the Lord spoke, and it came to be,
  the Lord commanded and it stood forth.
The Lord brings the counsel of nations to nothing
  and frustrates the plans of the peoples.

The counsel of the Lord stands forever,
  the thoughts of God's heart to all generations.
Blessed is the nation whose God is the Lord,
  the people whom the Lord has chosen as a
        heritage!

ANTIPHON THE THOUGHTS OF GOD'S HEART STAND
TO ALL GENERATIONS.

PSALM PRAYER
Let us pray (pause for quiet adoration):

Sacred Heart of Jesus,
how precious is your love for us.
Keep on loving those who know you
and hide us in the shadow of your cross
as we seek your mercy and your help
in our time of need.
You live and reign, now and for ever.
~AMEN.

READING   THE GOSPEL IN BRIEF   JOHN 3:16,35–36
God so loved the world that he gave his only Son,
so that everyone who believes in him may not
perish but may have eternal life. The Father loves
the Son and has placed all things in his hand.

Whoever believes in the Son has eternal life;
whoever disobeys the Son will not see life, but
must endure God's wrath.

Pause for Silent Adoration

RESPONSE

Take my yoke upon you and learn from me,
     alleluia!
~For I am meek and humble of heart, alleluia!

The Litany of the Sacred Heart of Jesus (see pages
226–229)

NOVENA PRAYER

Jesus, Savior of the world,
in your Holy Gospel you tell us:
"Ask, and it will be given you;
search, and you will find;
knock, and the door will be opened for you"
     (Matthew 7:7).
Moved by your divine promises,
I come before you to ask for
   (We name our needs).
I address you as my Savior,
whose heart is an inexhaustible source
   of grace and mercy.
Sacred Heart of Jesus,
friend of the human race,
consoler of the afflicted,
strength of those overwhelmed by their trials,

light of those who walk in darkness
or in the shadow of death,
I put my whole trust in you.
Blessed be Jesus Christ, true God and true man.
~Amen.

Sacred Heart of Jesus, have † mercy on me and
     mine.
~Amen.

A *public* novena often concludes with Benediction
of the Blessed Sacrament. See pages 104–106.

A Novena to the Precious Blood of Jesus

The precious blood of Jesus—poured out for us at his circumcision, in his agony in the Garden of Gethsemane, in his flogging and his crowning with thorns, on his blood-stained path to Golgotha, at his nailing to the cross, and as the Roman spear pierced his side—is a vivid depiction and sign of God's undying love for us. In every celebration of Mass Jesus says, "Take this, all of you, and drink from it: this is the cup of my blood, the blood of the new and everlasting covenant. Do this in memory of me."

The renowned Italian mystic and doctor of the Church, St. Catherine of Siena (1347–1380), encouraged everybody in the precious blood of Jesus that was shed on the Cross:

Since this holy cross is so sweet that it relieves all bitterness, pick it up for your journey along this road. For we pilgrim travelers need this holy wood for support until we have reached our destination, where our soul is at rest in our final home. How sweet to us now the burdens we have carried along the way! What peace, what calm, what sweetness our soul receives and enjoys once we have come home to port and have found the slain Lamb whom we had sought on the cross and who is now our table, our food, and our servant![93]

In the name of the Father, ✝ and of the Son, and of the Holy Spirit.

~AMEN.

Blessed be the most precious blood of Jesus.
~BY HIS WOUNDS WE HAVE BEEN HEALED.

HYMN

When I survey the wondrous Cross
Where the young Prince of Glory died,
My richest gain I count but loss,
And pour contempt on all my pride.

Forbid it, Lord, that I should boast
Save in the death of Christ, my God;
All the vain things that charm me most,
I sacrifice them to his blood.

See from his head, his hands, his feet,
Sorrow and love flow mingled down;
Did e'er such love and sorrow meet?
Or thorns compose so rich a crown?

His dying crimson like a robe
Spreads o'er his body on the Tree,
Then am I dead to all the globe,
And all the globe is dead to me.

Were the whole realm of nature mine,
That were a present far too small;
Love so amazing, so divine,
Demands my soul, my life, my all.[94]

PSALM 16:1, 5–11   A SONG OF THE LORD'S PASSION

ANTIPHON We are your people * BOUGHT WITH
THE PRICE OF YOUR OWN BLOOD.

Preserve me, O God, for in you I take refuge.
  I say to the Lord, "O Lord, you are my fortune,
    only you!"

The Lord is my chosen portion and my cup;
  you hold my lot.
The boundary lines have fallen for me in pleasant
    places;
  I have a goodly heritage.

I bless the Lord who gives me counsel;
  my heart also instructs me in the night.
I have set the Lord always before me;
  the Lord is at my right hand;
  I shall not be moved.

Therefore my heart is glad, and my soul rejoices;
  my body also dwells secure.
For you do not give me up to Sheol,
  or let your godly one see the Pit.

You show me the path of life;
  in your presence there is fullness of joy,
  in your right hand are pleasures for evermore.

ANTIPHON WE ARE YOUR PEOPLE * BOUGHT WITH
THE PRICE OF YOUR OWN BLOOD.

Psalm Prayer

Let us pray (pause for quiet adoration):

Abbà, dear Father,
by Christ's precious blood
the world is redeemed
and we are reconciled to you.
By the power of that same precious blood
defend us against all the evils of this life,
making peace by the blood of his cross.
We ask this through the same Christ our Lord.
~Amen.

Reading   Jesus, Our High Priest   1 Peter 1:18–20

You know that you were ransomed from the futile
ways inherited from your ancestors, not with
perishable things like silver or gold, but with the
precious blood of Christ, like a lamb without
defect or blemish. He was destined before the
foundation of the world, but was revealed at the
end of the ages for your sake.

Pause for Silent Adoration

Response

You have redeemed us with your blood, O Lord,
~and have made us a kingdom for our God.

LITANY OF THE PRECIOUS BLOOD
(pages 229–231)

NOVENA PRAYER

Lord Jesus, friend of the human race,
you shed your blood for us many times
during your life on earth.
As we offer the chalice of blessing
without ceasing on our altars,
forgive us our sins,
and remember us in all our needs,
especially *(We name our needs)*.
In virtue of your precious blood,
save us from the time of trial
and deliver us from the evil one.
You live and reign with the Father,
in the unity of the Holy Spirit,
one God, for ever and ever.
~AMEN.

May the precious plenty of Christ's precious blood
✝ wash us from all sin.
~AMEN.

A *public* novena often concludes with Benediction
of the Blessed Sacrament. See pages 104-106.

The Forty Hours Devotion

This public devotion known to the whole Catholic world is usually observed once a year by parishes on a schedule set by the bishop of the diocese. It maintains perpetual adoration of the Blessed Sacrament in the diocese and encourages Catholic parishioners to a renewed gratitude and reverence for the Blessed Sacrament. It is usually accompanied by sermons on the Real Presence and how we might best respect it and be thankful for it in our lives of prayer.

It is also a time of intercessory prayer with public litanies and a procession with the Blessed Sacrament. Many of the devotions in this book may be useful to those who practice private adoration during the Forty Hours.

Holy Thursday and Corpus Christi

On these two solemn days both processions and times of adoration are observed in several possible ways.

At the end of the Lord's Supper on Holy Thursday the celebrant and his ministers take the Host in procession to the altar of repose, and adoration is observed by the parish from that time until midnight.

In order to honor the Holy Eucharist more fully, the feast of Corpus Christi was initiated by Blessed Juliana of Cornillon in the city of Liege (Belgium) in 1246. In 1264 Pope Urban IV (1261–1264), a former archdeacon of Liege, invited St. Thomas Aquinas to compose a new liturgy for Corpus Christi and extended it to the whole Western church.

On the solemnity of Corpus Christi a solemn procession is often held outside church with several stations for prayer and blessing with the Sacrament.

The procession returns to the church for Benediction of the Blessed Sacrament, but if adoration continues throughout the day Benediction is deferred until the close of Evening Prayer.

Part 5
Litanies of
Intercession

Litanies are forms of popular intercessory prayer appropriate to public holy hours, novenas, nocturnal adoration, private times of adoration, and during processions of the Blessed Sacrament. Their prayerful rhythm brings home to us the wonderful attributes of our Savior and fills our hearts with beautiful phrases of spiritual longing and power. Litanies draw us into our Father's loving embrace and concentrate our minds and hearts on asking for our needs. They are particularly helpful as part of a holy hour or novena in a family or other group because of their repetitive petition/ answer format.

Jesus said to his disciples,
"Ask, and it will be given you;
Seek, and you will find;
Knock and the door will be opened to you."
Matthew 7:7–8

A Litany of the Holy Name of Jesus

Lord have mercy	~LORD HAVE MERCY
Christ have mercy	~CHRIST HAVE MERCY
Lord have mercy	~LORD HAVE MERCY
God the Father in heaven	~HAVE MERCY ON US
God the Son Redeemer of the world	~HAVE MERCY ON US
God the Holy Spirit	~HAVE MERCY ON US
Holy Trinity one God	~HAVE MERCY ON US
Jesus, Son of the living God	~HAVE MERCY ON US
Jesus, splendor of the Father	~HAVE MERCY ON US
Jesus, brightness of everlasting light	~HAVE MERCY ON US
Jesus, king of glory	~HAVE MERCY ON US
Jesus, dawn of justice	~HAVE MERCY ON US
Jesus, Son of the Virgin Mary	~HAVE MERCY ON US
Jesus, worthy of our love	~HAVE MERCY ON US
Jesus, worthy of our wonder	~HAVE MERCY ON US
Jesus, mighty God	~HAVE MERCY ON US
Jesus, father of the world to come	~HAVE MERCY ON US
Jesus, prince of peace	~HAVE MERCY ON US
Jesus, all-powerful	~HAVE MERCY ON US
Jesus, pattern of patience	~HAVE MERCY ON US
Jesus, model of obedience	~HAVE MERCY ON US
Jesus, gentle and humble of heart	~HAVE MERCY ON US
Jesus, lover of chastity	~HAVE MERCY ON US
Jesus, lover of us all	~HAVE MERCY ON US
Jesus, God of peace	~HAVE MERCY ON US
Jesus, author of life	~HAVE MERCY ON US
Jesus, model of goodness	~HAVE MERCY ON US
Jesus, seeker of souls	~HAVE MERCY ON US
Jesus, our God	~HAVE MERCY ON US
Jesus, our refuge	~HAVE MERCY ON US
Jesus, father of the poor	~HAVE MERCY ON US
Jesus, treasure of the faithful	~HAVE MERCY ON US

Jesus, good shepherd   ~HAVE MERCY ON US
Jesus, true light   ~HAVE MERCY ON US
Jesus, eternal wisdom   ~HAVE MERCY ON US
Jesus, infinite goodness   ~HAVE MERCY ON US
Jesus, our way and our life   ~HAVE MERCY ON US
Jesus, joy of angels   ~HAVE MERCY ON US
Jesus, king of patriarchs   ~HAVE MERCY ON US
Jesus, teacher of apostles   ~HAVE MERCY ON US
Jesus, master of evangelists ~HAVE MERCY ON US
Jesus, courage of martyrs   ~HAVE MERCY ON US
Jesus, light of confessors   ~HAVE MERCY ON US
Jesus, purity of virgins   ~HAVE MERCY ON US
Jesus, crown of all saints   ~HAVE MERCY ON US

Lord be merciful   ~JESUS SAVE YOUR PEOPLE
From all evil   ~JESUS SAVE YOUR PEOPLE
From every sin   ~JESUS SAVE YOUR PEOPLE
From the snares of the devil ~JESUS SAVE YOUR PEOPLE
From your anger   ~JESUS SAVE YOUR PEOPLE
From the spirit of infidelity ~JESUS SAVE YOUR PEOPLE
From everlasting death   ~JESUS SAVE YOUR PEOPLE
From neglect of your
    Holy Spirit   ~JESUS SAVE YOUR PEOPLE

By the mystery of your
    incarnation   ~JESUS SAVE YOUR PEOPLE
By your birth   ~JESUS SAVE YOUR PEOPLE
By your childhood   ~JESUS SAVE YOUR PEOPLE
By your hidden life   ~JESUS SAVE YOUR PEOPLE
By your public ministry   ~JESUS SAVE YOUR PEOPLE
By your agony and
    crucifixion   ~JESUS SAVE YOUR PEOPLE
By your abandonment   ~JESUS SAVE YOUR PEOPLE
By your grief and sorrow   ~JESUS SAVE YOUR PEOPLE
By your death and burial   ~JESUS SAVE YOUR PEOPLE
By your rising to new life   ~JESUS SAVE YOUR PEOPLE

A Litany of the Holy Name of Jesus **225**

By your return in glory to the Father	~JESUS SAVE YOUR PEOPLE
By your gift of the holy Eucharist	~JESUS SAVE YOUR PEOPLE
By your joy and glory	~JESUS SAVE YOUR PEOPLE
Christ hear us	~CHRIST HEAR US
Lord Jesus hear our prayer	~LORD JESUS HEAR OUR PRAYER
Lamb of God you take away the sins of the world	~HAVE MERCY ON US
Lamb of God you take away the sins of the world	~HAVE MERCY ON US
Lamb of God you take away the sins of the world	~HAVE MERCY ON US

Let us pray:
Lord, may we who honor the holy name of Jesus enjoy his friendship in this life and be filled with eternal joy in the kingdom where he lives and reigns for ever and ever.
~AMEN.[95]

A Litany of the Sacred Heart of Jesus

Lord, have mercy	~LORD, HAVE MERCY
Christ, have mercy	~CHRIST, HAVE MERCY
Lord, have mercy	~LORD, HAVE MERCY
God our Father in heaven,	~HAVE MERCY ON US
God the Son, Redeemer of the world	~HAVE MERCY ON US
God the Holy Spirit	~HAVE MERCY ON US
Holy Trinity, one God	~HAVE MERCY ON US

Heart of Jesus, Son of the
eternal Father ~HAVE MERCY ON US
Heart of Jesus, formed by the Holy Spirit
in the womb of the Virgin Mother ~HAVE MERCY ON US
Heart of Jesus, one with the
eternal Word ~HAVE MERCY ON US
Heart of Jesus, infinite in majesty ~HAVE MERCY ON US
Heart of Jesus, holy temple of God ~HAVE MERCY ON US
Heart of Jesus, tabernacle of the
Most High ~HAVE MERCY ON US
Heart of Jesus, house of God
and gate of heaven ~HAVE MERCY ON US
Heart of Jesus, aflame with love
for us ~HAVE MERCY ON US
Heart of Jesus, source of justice
and love ~HAVE MERCY ON US
Heart of Jesus, full of goodness
and love ~HAVE MERCY ON US
Heart of Jesus, well-spring of
all virtue ~HAVE MERCY ON US
Heart of Jesus, worthy of all praise ~HAVE MERCY ON US
Heart of Jesus, king and center
of all hearts ~HAVE MERCY ON US
Heart of Jesus, treasure-house
of wisdom and knowledge ~HAVE MERCY ON US
Heart of Jesus, in whom there
dwells the fullness of God ~HAVE MERCY ON US
Heart of Jesus, in whom the
Father is well pleased ~HAVE MERCY ON US
Heart of Jesus, of whose fullness
we have all received ~HAVE MERCY ON US
Heart of Jesus, desire of the
everlasting hills ~HAVE MERCY ON US

Heart of Jesus, patient and
full of mercy   ~HAVE MERCY ON US
Heart of Jesus, generous to all
who turn to you   ~HAVE MERCY ON US
Heart of Jesus, fountain of life
and holiness   ~HAVE MERCY ON US
Heart of Jesus, atonement for
our sins   ~HAVE MERCY ON US
Heart of Jesus, overwhelmed
with insults   ~HAVE MERCY ON US
Heart of Jesus, broken for our sins   ~HAVE MERCY ON US
Heart of Jesus, obedient even
to death   ~HAVE MERCY ON US
Heart of Jesus, pierced by a lance   ~HAVE MERCY ON US
Heart of Jesus, source of all
consolation   ~HAVE MERCY ON US
Heart of Jesus, our life and
resurrection   ~HAVE MERCY ON US
Heart of Jesus, our peace and
reconciliation   ~HAVE MERCY ON US
Heart of Jesus, victim for our sins   ~HAVE MERCY ON US
Heart of Jesus, salvation of all
who trust in you   ~HAVE MERCY ON US
Heart of Jesus, hope of all who
die in you   ~HAVE MERCY ON US
Heart of Jesus, delight of all the
saints   ~HAVE MERCY ON US

Lamb of God, you take away
the sins of the world   ~HAVE MERCY ON US
Lamb of God, you take away
the sins of the world   ~HAVE MERCY ON US
Lamb of God, you take away
the sins of the world   ~HAVE MERCY ON US

Jesus, gentle and humble
of heart   ~TOUCH OUR HEARTS AND MAKE
                  THEM LIKE YOUR OWN

Let us pray:

Father,
we rejoice in the gifts of love
we have received from the heart of Jesus your Son.
Open our hearts to share his life
and continue to bless us with his love.
We ask this in the name of Jesus the Lord.
~AMEN.[96]

A Litany of the
Precious Blood of Jesus

Lord, have mercy	~LORD, HAVE MERCY
Christ, have mercy	~CHRIST, HAVE MERCY
Lord, have mercy	~LORD, HAVE MERCY
God our Father in heaven	~HAVE MERCY ON US
God the Son, Redeemer of the world	~HAVE MERCY ON US
God the Holy Spirit	~HAVE MERCY ON US
Holy Trinity, one God	~HAVE MERCY ON US
Blood of Christ, only Son of the Father	~BE OUR SALVATION
Blood of Christ, incarnate Word	~BE OUR SALVATION
Blood of Christ, of the new and eternal covenant	~BE OUR SALVATION
Blood of Christ, that spilled to the ground	~BE OUR SALVATION

Blood of Christ, that flowed at the
    scourging   ~BE OUR SALVATION
Blood of Christ, dripping from
    the thorns   ~BE OUR SALVATION
Blood of Christ, shed on the cross   ~BE OUR SALVATION
Blood of Christ, the price of our
    redemption   ~BE OUR SALVATION
Blood of Christ, our only claim
    to pardon   ~BE OUR SALVATION
Blood of Christ, our blessing cup   ~BE OUR SALVATION
Blood of Christ, in which we are
    washed   ~BE OUR SALVATION
Blood of Christ, torrent of mercy   ~BE OUR SALVATION
Blood of Christ, that overcomes evil   ~BE OUR SALVATION
Blood of Christ, strength of the
    martyrs   ~BE OUR SALVATION
Blood of Christ, endurance of the
    saints   ~BE OUR SALVATION
Blood of Christ, that makes the
    barren fruitful   ~BE OUR SALVATION
Blood of Christ, protection of the
    threatened   ~BE OUR SALVATION
Blood of Christ, comfort of the
    weary   ~BE OUR SALVATION
Blood of Christ, solace of the
    mourner   ~BE OUR SALVATION
Blood of Christ, hope of the
    repentant   ~BE OUR SALVATION
Blood of Christ, consolation
    of the dying   ~BE OUR SALVATION
Blood of Christ, our peace and
    refreshment   ~BE OUR SALVATION
Blood of Christ, our pledge of life   ~BE OUR SALVATION

Blood of Christ, by which we pass
to glory   ~BE OUR SALVATION

Blood of Christ, most worthy of
honor   ~BE OUR SALVATION

Lamb of God, you take away
the sins of the world   ~HAVE MERCY ON US

Lamb of God, you take away
the sins of the world   ~HAVE MERCY ON US

Lamb of God, you take away
the sins of the world   ~HAVE MERCY ON US

Lord, you redeemed us
by your blood   ~YOU HAVE MADE US A KINGDOM
                                  TO SERVE OUR GOD

Let us pray:

Father,
by the blood of your Son
you have set us free and saved us from death.
Continue your work of love within us,
that by constantly celebrating the mystery of our
salvation
we may reach the eternal life it promises.
We ask this through Christ our Lord.
~AMEN.[97]

A Litany of the Love of God

Lord, have mercy.   ~LORD, HAVE MERCY.
Christ, have mercy.   ~CHRIST, HAVE MERCY.
Lord, have mercy.   ~LORD, HAVE MERCY.

God our Father in heaven,	~HAVE MERCY ON US.
God the Son, Redeemer of the world,	~HAVE MERCY ON US.
God the Holy Spirit,	~HAVE MERCY ON US.
Holy Trinity, one God,	~HAVE MERCY ON US.

Infinite Love,	~I LOVE YOU.
You who first loved me,	~I LOVE YOU.
You who commanded me to love you,	~I LOVE YOU.
With all my heart,	~I LOVE YOU.
With all my soul,	~I LOVE YOU.
With all my mind,	~I LOVE YOU.
With all my strength,	~I LOVE YOU.

Above all possessions and honor,	~I LOVE YOU.
Above all pleasures and enjoyments,	~I LOVE YOU.
More than myself and all that belongs to me,	~I LOVE YOU.
More than all my relatives and friends,	~I LOVE YOU.
More than all human beings and angels,	~I LOVE YOU.
Above all created things in heaven and earth,	~I LOVE YOU.

Only for yourself,	~I LOVE YOU.
Because you are the Sovereign Good,	~I LOVE YOU.
Because you are infinitely worthy of being loved,	~I LOVE YOU.
Because you are infinitely perfect,	~I LOVE YOU.
Even if you had not promised me heaven,	~I LOVE YOU.
Even if you had not warned me of hell,	~I LOVE YOU.
Even if you try me by want and misfortune,	~I LOVE YOU.
In wealth and in poverty,	~I LOVE YOU.
In prosperity and in adversity,	~I LOVE YOU.
In health and in sickness,	~I LOVE YOU.
In life and in death,	~I LOVE YOU.
In time and in eternity,	~I LOVE YOU.

In union with that love by which all
the saints
and angels love you in heaven,   ~I LOVE YOU.
In union with that love by which the
Blessed Virgin Mary loves you,   ~I LOVE YOU.
In union with that love by which you love
yourself eternally,   ~I LOVE YOU.

You are just, O Lord,
in all your ways,   ~AND LOVING IN ALL YOUR DEEDS.

PRAYER
Mighty love of God,
overflowing into creation
and into every created order:
Bring us up before the great white throne
where, in profound awe and reverence,
we shall enjoy all goodness and peace
at the heart of the Blessed Trinity.
We ask this through Christ our Lord.
~AMEN.[98]

A Byzantine Litany

Most of the litanies that we know come from the heritage of the Latin or Western Church. This expressive litany derives from the Great Church of the Byzantine Empire and its many dependencies in Greece, Russia, Romania, Bulgaria, Serbia, Palestine, and now even from North American churches of the Byzantine rite and tradition.

In peace, let us pray to the Lord.   ~LORD, HAVE MERCY.

For peace from on high and for the salvation of our souls,
  let us pray to the Lord.   ~LORD HAVE MERCY.

For peace throughout the world, the welfare of God's
  Church, and the unity of the human race,
  let us pray to the Lord.   ~LORD HAVE MERCY.

For this holy place and for those who enter it with faith,
  reverence, and fear of God, let us pray to the Lord.
                                    ~LORD HAVE MERCY.

For our holy father, Name, for our bishop, Name,
  for our pastor, Name, and for all the clergy and people,
  let us pray to the Lord.   ~LORD HAVE MERCY.

For this nation, its government, and all who serve and
    protect us, let us pray to the Lord. ~LORD HAVE MERCY.

For this city and for every place of human habitation,
  and for all those living in them,
  let us pray to the Lord.   ~LORD HAVE MERCY.

For seasonable weather, bountiful harvests,
  and for peaceful times, let us pray to the Lord.

                                    ~LORD HAVE MERCY.

For the safety of travelers, the recovery of the sick,
the deliverance of the oppressed, and the release of
    prisoners, let us pray to the Lord. ~LORD HAVE MERCY.

For our deliverance from all affliction, hostility, danger,
    and need, let us pray to the Lord. ~LORD HAVE MERCY.

Help, save, pity, and defend us, O God,
  by your grace.   ~LORD HAVE MERCY.

Pause for our special intentions.

As we rejoice in the communion of the Blessed Virgin
   Mary, and of all the saints, let us commend ourselves,
   one another, and our whole life to Christ our Lord.
                                        ~To you, O Lord.

PRAYER

Almighty God and Father,
by your grace we make these prayers with one
        accord,
relying on your promise
that where two or three are gathered together in
        your name
you will stand in their midst.
Please grant that what may be best for us,
knowledge of your truth in this world,
and life everlasting in the age to come.
We ask this through Christ our Lord.
~AMEN.

A Litany of the Resurrection

This is another brilliant litany of the Byzantine churches
that is used during Eastertide.

In peace, let us pray to the Lord.   ~LORD, HAVE MERCY.

For peace from on high, and for the salvation of our souls,
   let us pray to the Lord.   ~LORD, HAVE MERCY.

That the Lord Jesus Christ, our Savior, may grant us
   triumph and victory over the temptations of our visible
   and invisible enemies,
      let us pray to the Lord.   ~LORD, HAVE MERCY.

That He may crush beneath our feet the prince of
   darkness and his powers,
      let us pray to the Lord. ~LORD, HAVE MERCY.

That he may raise us up with Him, and make us
   rise from the tomb of our sins and offenses,
      let us pray to the Lord. ~LORD, HAVE MERCY.

That He may purify us, and make us shine with the glory
   of His holy resurrection,
      let us pray to the Lord. ~LORD, HAVE MERCY.

That we may deserve the grace of entering into the
   chamber of his divine wedding-feast, and to rejoice
   beyond words, together with His heavenly attendants
   and the hosts of the saints glorified through Him in the
      Church Triumphant,
      let us pray to the Lord. ~LORD, HAVE MERCY.

That we may be delivered from all affliction, wrath,
   danger, and need,
      let us pray to the Lord. ~LORD, HAVE MERCY.

Help us, save us, have mercy on us, and protect us, O God,
   by your grace. ~LORD, HAVE MERCY.

Let us remember the all-holy, spotless, most highly
   blessed, and glorious Lady, the Mother of God and
   ever-virgin Mary, and all the saints, and commend
   ourselves, one another, and our whole life to Christ our
   God. ~TO YOU, O LORD.

For You are our Light and our Resurrection, O Christ
   God;
   and we send up glory to You, and to Your eternal Father,
   and to Your all-holy, good, and life-giving Spirit, now
   and always, and for ever and ever. ~AMEN.[99]

A Litany of the Beatitudes

Lord Jesus, teacher of righteousness;
~GIVE US TRUE HAPPINESS AND EVERY BLESSING.

Bless the poor and humble in spirit;
~MAKE THEM INHERIT THE KINGDOM OF HEAVEN.

Bless those who mourn for lost blessings;
~BE THEIR COMFORT IN TIME OF TROUBLE.

Bless those who are meek and humble of heart;
~LET THEM INHERIT WHAT GOD HAS PROMISED.

Bless those who hunger and thirst for what God
    requires;
~AND FILL THEM WITH DIVINE WHOLENESS.

Bless those who are merciful towards others;
~MAY GOD BE MERCIFUL TO THEM IN TURN.

Bless those who are pure in heart;
~LET THEM SEE GOD IN THE LIGHT OF GLORY.

Bless those who make peace on earth;
~AND CALL THEM THE CHILDREN OF GOD.

Bless those who are persecuted for being holy;
~GIVE THEM POSSESSION OF THE KINGDOM OF
    GOD.

Bless those who are slandered and insulted for
    your sake;
~MAKE THEM HAPPY AND GLAD, FOR THEIR
    REWARD
  IS GREAT IN THEIR HEAVENLY HOME.

Pause for our special intentions.

Lord Jesus, light of the world,
you taught us how to be happy
in this life and in the next,
by walking in your blessed footsteps:
Make us humble, pure, and merciful;
help us to make peace and pursue holiness,
and to rejoice when we are persecuted,
slandered, and insulted for your sake.
Illumine our hearts with your sacred teaching,
O Savior of the world,
and form us as your devout disciples
and the children of God your Father,
to the glory of your holy name.
~AMEN.

A Litany of the Seven Gifts of the Spirit

Come, Spirit of Wisdom, and give us a taste
   for things divine:
~COME, HOLY SPIRIT!

Come, Spirit of Understanding, and show us
      everything in the light of eternity:
~COME, HOLY SPIRIT!

Come, Spirit of Counsel, and direct our hearts and
      minds toward our heavenly home:
~COME, HOLY SPIRIT!

Come, Spirit of Might, and strengthen us
   against every evil inclination:
~COME, HOLY SPIRIT!

Come, Spirit of Knowledge, and lift our hearts on
      high:
~COME, HOLY SPIRIT!

Come, Spirit of Godliness, and fill us with the love
      of God and our neighbor:
~COME, HOLY SPIRIT!

Come, Spirit of Awe before the majesty of God,
   and make us tremble with respect and
      reverence before the Holy and Undivided
      Trinity:
~COME, HOLY SPIRIT!

When you send forth your Spirit they are created
~AND YOU RENEW THE FACE OF THE EARTH.

Let us pray:

Holy Spirit of God,
final gift of our blessed Savior
as he ascended into heaven:
Pour out the seven gifts on your Church,
renew and refresh it for service,
and inspire each one of us anew
as we walk with Jesus
under the mighty hand of God.
Blessed be God, now and for ever!
~AMEN.

A Litany of the
Blessed Virgin Mary (Loreto)

Lord, have mercy	~LORD, HAVE MERCY
Christ, have mercy	~CHRIST, HAVE MERCY
Lord, have mercy	~LORD, HAVE MERCY
God our Father in heaven,	~HAVE MERCY ON US
God the Son, Redeemer of the world	~HAVE MERCY ON US
God the Holy Spirit	~HAVE MERCY ON US
Holy Trinity, one God	~HAVE MERCY ON US
Holy Mary	~PRAY FOR US
Holy Mother of God	~PRAY FOR US
Most honored of virgins	~PRAY FOR US
Mother of Christ	~PRAY FOR US
Mother of the Church	~PRAY FOR US
Mother of divine grace	~PRAY FOR US
Mother most pure	~PRAY FOR US
Mother of chaste love	~PRAY FOR US
Mother and virgin	~PRAY FOR US
Sinless Mother	~PRAY FOR US
Dearest of mothers	~PRAY FOR US
Model of motherhood	~PRAY FOR US
Mother of good counsel	~PRAY FOR US
Mother of our Creator	~PRAY FOR US
Mother of our Savior	~PRAY FOR US
Virgin most wise	~PRAY FOR US
Virgin rightly praised	~PRAY FOR US
Virgin rightly renowned	~PRAY FOR US
Virgin most powerful	~PRAY FOR US
Virgin gentle in mercy	~PRAY FOR US
Faithful virgin	~PRAY FOR US

Mirror of justice	~PRAY FOR US
Throne of wisdom	~PRAY FOR US
Cause of our joy	~PRAY FOR US
Shrine of the Spirit	~PRAY FOR US
Glory of Israel	~PRAY FOR US
Vessel of selfless devotion	~PRAY FOR US
Mystical rose	~PRAY FOR US
Tower of David	~PRAY FOR US
Tower of ivory	~PRAY FOR US
House of gold	~PRAY FOR US
Ark of the covenant	~PRAY FOR US
Gate of heaven	~PRAY FOR US
Morning Star	~PRAY FOR US
Health of the sick	~PRAY FOR US
Refuge of sinners	~PRAY FOR US
Comfort of the troubled	~PRAY FOR US
Help of Christians	~PRAY FOR US
Queen of angels	~PRAY FOR US
Queen of patriarchs and prophets	~PRAY FOR US
Queen of apostles and martyrs	~PRAY FOR US
Queen of confessors and virgins	~PRAY FOR US
Queen of all saints	~PRAY FOR US
Queen conceived in grace	~PRAY FOR US
Queen raised up to glory	~PRAY FOR US
Queen of the rosary	~PRAY FOR US
Queen of the family	~PRAY FOR US
Queen of peace	~PRAY FOR US
Lamb of God, you take away the sins of the world	~HAVE MERCY ON US
Lamb of God, you take away the sins of the world	~HAVE MERCY ON US

Lamb of God, you take away
the sins of the world   ~HAVE MERCY ON US

Pray for us, holy
Mother of God   ~THAT WE MAY BECOME WORTHY
OF THE PROMISES OF CHRIST

Let us pray:

Eternal God,
let your people enjoy constant health in mind and
body.
Through the intercession of the Virgin Mary
free us from the sorrows of this life
and lead us to happiness in the life to come.
Grant this through Christ our Lord.
~AMEN.[100]

A Litany of Saint Joseph

Lord, have mercy   ~LORD, HAVE MERCY
Christ, have mercy   ~CHRIST, HAVE MERCY
Lord, have mercy   ~LORD, HAVE MERCY

God our Father in heaven   ~HAVE MERCY ON US
God the Son, Redeemer of the
world   ~HAVE MERCY ON US
God the Holy Spirit   ~HAVE MERCY ON US
Holy Trinity, one God   ~HAVE MERCY ON US

Saint Joseph   ~PRAY FOR US
Noble son of the House of David   ~PRAY FOR US
Light of patriarchs   ~PRAY FOR US
Husband of the Mother of God   ~PRAY FOR US
Guardian of the Virgin   ~PRAY FOR US

Foster father of the Son of God	~PRAY FOR US
Faithful guardian of Christ	~PRAY FOR US
Head of the holy family	~PRAY FOR US
Joseph, chaste and just,	~PRAY FOR US
Joseph, prudent and brave,	~PRAY FOR US
Joseph, obedient and loyal,	~PRAY FOR US
Pattern of patience	~PRAY FOR US
Lover of poverty	~PRAY FOR US
Model of workers	~PRAY FOR US
Example to parents	~PRAY FOR US
Guardian of virgins	~PRAY FOR US
Pillar of family life	~PRAY FOR US
Comfort of the troubled	~PRAY FOR US
Hope of the sick	~PRAY FOR US
Patron of the dying	~PRAY FOR US
Terror of evil spirits	~PRAY FOR US
Protector of the Church	~PRAY FOR US

Lamb of God, you take away the sins of the world	~HAVE MERCY ON US
Lamb of God, you take away the sins of the world	~HAVE MERCY ON US
Lamb of God, you take away the sins of the world	~HAVE MERCY ON US

God made him master of his household	~AND PUT HIM IN CHARGE OF ALL THAT HE OWNED

Let us pray:

Almighty God,
in your infinite wisdom and love
you chose Joseph to be the husband of Mary,
the mother of your Son.

As we enjoy his protection on earth
may we have the help of his prayers in heaven.
We ask this through Christ our Lord.
~AMEN.[101]

Part 6
Devotions to the Blessed Virgin Mary

Jesus' Father is our Father and his Mother is our Mother. The coming of the eternal Word of God in the womb of Mary signals the perfect conjunction of the human and the divine and unites us by grace to the Holy and Undivided Trinity. Devotion to the Mother of God is at the heart of the Catholic faith and recognizes her as "our life, our sweetness, and our hope" *(Salve Regina)*. Let us turn to her for protection She listens to our prayers and helps us in all our needs. *(Sub tuum praesidium).*

Devotion to Mary is the normal accompaniment to devotion to Jesus in the Blessed Sacrament. It was she who gave Jesus his body and blood, the same body and blood that is our sacramental food. She is indeed Our Lady of the Blessed Sacrament. She prays with us and for us as we adore her son in the tabernacle.

May the Virgin Mary encourage and lead us to meet her Son in the Eucharistic Mystery. May Mary, the real Ark of the Covenant, teach us to frequent her Son Jesus in the tabernacle with purity, humility, and devotion. May she who is the "Star of Evangelization" sustain us in our pilgrimage of faith to bring the Light of Christ to all human beings and to all nations.

Pope John Paul II (1920–2005)[102]

Ave, verum corpus

Hail to thee! true Body sprung
From the Virgin Mary's womb!
The same that on the cross was hung,
And bore for us the bitter doom.

Thou whose side was pierced and flowed
Both with water and with blood,
Suffer us to taste of thee
In our life's long agony.

O kind, O loving One!
O sweet Jesus, Mary's Son.

From the Tridentine Liturgy

Listen to Mary:

Let us take our place, dear brothers and sisters, at the school of the saints, who are the great interpreters of true Eucharistic piety. In them the theology of the Eucharist takes on all the splendor of a lived reality; it becomes "contagious" and, in a manner of speaking, it "warms our hearts." Above all, let us listen to Mary, Most Holy, in whom the Eucharist appears, more than in anyone else, as a mystery of light. Gazing upon Mary, we come to know the transforming power present in the Eucharist.

In her we see the world renewed in love. Contemplating her, assumed body and soul into heaven, we see opening up before us those "new heavens" and a "new earth" which will appear at the second coming of Christ. Here below, the Eucharist represents their pledge, and in a certain way, their anticipation: "Come, Lord Jesus!" (Revelation 22:20).

Pope John Paul II (1920–2005)[103]

The Canticle of Mary (Luke 1:46–55)
Like our Lord's Sermon of the Mount, Mary's *Magnificat* upsets all worldly values: a lowly woman, Mary, is blessed by all generations; the proud and arrogant, the tyrants, the rich are set down; the poor, the humble, the lowly, the hungry are exalted. Let us stand with her and all her values.

My soul proclaims the greatness of the Lord,
my spirit rejoices in God my Savior,
for you, Lord, have looked with favor on your
    lowly servant.

From this day all generations will call me blessed:
  you, the Almighty, have done great things for me
  and holy is your name.
  You have mercy on those who fear you,
  from generation to generation.

You have shown strength with your arm
and scattered the proud in their conceit,
casting down the mighty from their thrones
and lifting up the lowly.

You have filled the hungry with good things
and sent the rich away empty.

You have come to the aid of your servant Israel,
to remember the promise of mercy,
the promise made to our forebears,
to Abraham and his children for ever.

PRAYER

Let us put our complete trust in Mary:

Holy Mother of God,
you are our model of faith
and of complete submission to the Father.
By your faith, trust, and obedience,
and by your fervent prayers of intercession,
give us all the virtues displayed in your life of
        faith
and draw us close to your immaculate heart
that worships our God with such perfection.
Blest be the great Mother of God, Mary most holy!
~AMEN.

St. Bernardine of Siena (1380–1444)[104]

Sub tuum praesidium

This is the earliest surviving prayer to Mary, probably
of Egyptian origin, late second century. Pope Paul VI
referred to it as "the well-known prayer *Sub tuum
praesidium*, venerable for its antiquity and admirable
for its content."[105]

We turn to you for protection,
holy Mother of God.
Listen to our prayers
and help us in our needs.
Save us from every danger,
glorious and blessed Virgin.[106]

To Mary

Mary, dear mother, who gave God birth,
Help and care for us living here on earth.
  Govern, give us knowledge, and advise.
Since you're our mother too, maiden and wife,
Bathe away our sin; grant us good life
  And, in every need, help us to be wise.[107]

The Infant and the Altar

" [At Christmas] you too will find the Infant
today wrapped in swaddling clothes and laid on
the manger of the altar. Take care that His mean
apparel does not disturb the gaze of your faith or
lessen your reverence for the Body that you behold
in another form. For just as Mary, his Mother,
wrapped Him in swaddling clothes, so grace as a
mother conceals from us the reality of this same
sacred Body under another species and wisdom as
a mother covers the mysteries and majesty of the
Divine Word under symbols and figures."

Blessed Guerric of Igny († 1157)[108]

A Salutation to the Blessed Virgin

St. Francis, "a truly Catholic and apostolic man," built his personal life of prayer by a deep and warm devotion to the Mother of God.

Hail, holy Lady,
    Most holy Queen,
    Mary, Mother of God,
    Ever Virgin;
Chosen by the most holy Father in heaven,
    Consecrated by him,
    With his most holy beloved Son
    And the Holy Spirit, the Comforter.
On you descended and in you still remains
    All the fullness of grace
    And every good.
Hail, his Palace!
Hail, his Tabernacle!
Hail, his Home!
Hail, his Robe!
Hail, his Handmaid!
Hail, his Mother!
And, hail all holy virtues,
    Who, by the grace
    And inspiration of the Holy Spirit
    Are poured into the hearts of the faithful
    So that, faithless no longer,
    They may be made faithful servants of God
    Through you.

St. Francis of Assisi (1181–1226)[109]

Antiphon of St. Francis
St. Francis prayed this supremely Trinitarian prayer to Mary before beginning each "hour" of the Liturgy of the Hours.

Holy Virgin Mary,
among all the women of the world,
there is none like you:
you are the daughter and the handmaid
of the most high King and Father of heaven;
you are the mother of our most holy Lord Jesus
      Christ;
you are the spouse of the Holy Spirit.
Pray for us with Saint Michael the Archangel
and all the powers of the heavens and all the saints
to your most holy and beloved Son, our Lord and
      Master.

St. Francis of Assisi (1181–1226)[110]

Memorare
Remember, most loving Virgin Mary,
never was it heard
that anyone who turned to you for help
was left unaided.
Inspired by this confidence,
though burdened by my sins,
I run to you for protection.
Mother of the Word of God,
do not despise my words of pleading
but be merciful and hear my prayer. Amen.[111]

A Novena to Our Sorrowful Mother

Our Lady of Sorrows standing at the foot of the cross is our great advocate in all our needs and especially when we need comfort and compassion. Her many shrines in North America served by the Servite Order are testimonies to the fact that she will "help us in our needs and save us from every danger" *(Sub tuum praesidium)*.

ANTIPHON

Old Simeon said to Mary, *

"THIS CHILD IS DESTINED FOR THE FALLING AND RISING OF MANY IN ISRAEL, AND TO BE A SIGN THAT WILL BE OPPOSED SO THAT THE INNER THOUGHTS OF MANY WILL BE REVEALED—AND A SWORD WILL PIERCE YOUR OWN SOUL TOO."
Luke 2:34

A Roman soldier opened Jesus' side with his spear,
~AND PIERCED THE HEART OF HIS MOTHER.

Let us pray to our Lady of Sorrows:

Mary, Mother of Sorrows,
you experienced the poverty,
the rejection, and the misunderstanding
that was Jesus' fate.
As he hung on the cross,
you stood at his side
and watched him writhe in pain
and knew the desolation that wrung his soul.
By his precious blood and your tears,

stand at our side as we feel
some of the pressures and pains
that weigh on our lives in this world.
Be with us in trials and tribulations,
and hear our special prayers (We state our needs).
Holy Mother of God be our mother too,
now and always and for ever and ever.
~Amen.

May the glorious passion of our Lord Jesus Christ
✝ bring us to the joys of paradise.
~Amen.

A Novena to Our Lady of Guadalupe

In the Western hemisphere the preeminent devotion
to St. Mary is centered on the shrine of Guadalupe in
Mexico City. Millions journey there each year to present
their burdens to the Mother of Mercy. In a very special
way she is the protector of the poor and oppressed, the
comforter of the afflicted, the refuge of sinners, and the
help of Christians.

Blessed be the great Mother of God, Mary most
    holy.
~Blessed be the name of Mary, virgin and
    mother.

Hymn

Hail, our Queen and Mother blest!
Joy when all was sadness,
life and hope you brought to earth,
Mother of our gladness.

Children of the sinful Eve,
sinless Eve befriend us,
exiled in this vale of tears:
strength and comfort send us.

Pray for us, O Patroness,
be our consolation!
Lead us home to see your Son,
Jesus, our salvation!

Gracious are you, full of grace,
loving as none other;
joy of heaven and joy of earth,
Mary, God's own Mother!
Salve Regina[112]

READING **QUEEN MARY** **REVELATION 12:1**

A great sign appeared in heaven: a woman clothed
with the sun, with the moon under her feet, and
on her head a crown of twelve stars.

RESPONSORY

Mary, you are more worthy of honor than the
    cherubim,
~AND FAR MORE GLORIOUS THAN THE SERAPHIM.

LITANY OF THE BLESSED VIRGIN MARY
(pages 240–242)

Novena Prayer

Remember, most loving Virgin Mary,
never was it heard
that anyone who turned to you for help
was left unaided.
Inspired by this confidence,
though burdened by my sins,
I run to you for protection
for you are my mother (We state our needs).
Mother of the Word of God,
do not despise my words of pleading
but be merciful and hear my prayer.[113]

Closing Prayer

God of power and mercy,
you blessed the Americas at Tepeyac
with the presence of the Virgin Mary of
　　　Guadalupe.
May her prayers help all men and women
to accept each other as brothers and sisters.
Through your justice present in our hearts
may social justice and peace reign in the world.
Please grant this through Christ our Lord.
~Amen.[114]

Saint Juan Diego, the visionary of Tepeyac,
~Pray for us.

May the Virgin Mary of Guadalupe
✝ be the joy and consolation of her people.
~Amen.

Te Matrem Laudamus

We praise you as our Mother,
    we acclaim you as our blessed Lady.
All the earth reveres you,
    the Eternal Father's daughter.

The hosts of heaven and all the angelic powers
    sing your praise:
the angels join in the dance,
the archangels applaud, the virtues give praise,
the principalities rejoice, the powers exult,
the dominations delight, the thrones make
      festival,
the cherubim and seraphim cry out unceasingly:

> *Holy, holy, holy is the great Mother of God,*
>   *Mary most holy;*
> *Jesus, the blessed fruit of your womb,*
>   *is the glory of heaven and earth.*

The glorious choir of apostles,
    the noble company of prophets,
    the white-robed army of martyrs,
    all sing your praise.

The holy church throughout the world celebrates
      you:
    the daughter of infinite Majesty,
    the mother of God's true and only Son,
  the bride of the Spirit of truth and consolation.

You bore Christ, the King of glory,
  the eternal Son of the Father.
When he took our nature to set us free,
  he did not spurn your virgin womb.

When he overcame death's sting,
  he assumed you into heaven.
You now sit with your Son
  at God's right hand in glory.

Intercede for us, O Virgin Mary,
  when he comes to be our judge.
Help your chosen people,
  bought with his precious blood.
And bring us with all the saints
  into glory everlasting.

Save your people, holy Virgin,
  and bless your inheritance.
Rule them and uphold them,
  now and for ever.

Day by day we salute you;
  we acclaim you unceasingly.
In your goodness pray for us sinners;
  have mercy on us poor sinners.

May your mercy sustain us always,
  for we put our trust in you.
In you, dear Mother, do we trust;
  defend us now and for ever. Amen.[115]

Part 7
The Rosary before the Blessed Sacrament

For many adorers no devotion before the Blessed Sacrament is more appropriate than the Rosary of our Blessed Lady. Meditating on the twenty mysteries of our Lord's life before the living Jesus in the Sacrament of the Altar combine, in one movement of prayer, concentration on the Jesus of the Gospel text and on the beauty on the face of Christ in the Mystery of Faith.

The Rosary is a Christological and Marian devotion that presents the chief mysteries of the life of Jesus for our prayerful meditation. It first appeared in the cloisters of the Carthusian hermits in the fifteenth century but was preached throughout Europe by the Order of Preachers (Dominicans), who in Ireland were commonly called "the Fathers of the Rosary." It soon won papal approval and the new religious orders of the Catholic Reformation (especially the Jesuits) spread it far and wide across the Catholic world.

In our time Pope John Paul II (1920–2005) began a powerful renewal of the Rosary as it was originally intended and designed, and added the five luminous mysteries to the original fifteen.[116]

The Rosary contains four groups of five mysteries each: joyous, luminous, sorrowful, and glorious. Each decade of the rosary is composed of one Our Father, ten Hail Marys, and one Gloria Patri. A prayer summarizes each decade and a Marian anthem completes each of the four sets of mysteries.

The use of rosary beads is a useful counter and sets up a peaceful rhythm favorable to personal, meditative prayer on the twenty mysteries.

Suggestions for Praying the Rosary

1. Read the key Bible passage presented here before each decade and pause briefly for silent meditation before beginning the vocal prayers.
2. Pray the vocal prayers with care and devotion, respecting the punctuation and structure of each prayer, and praying without haste!
3. Add a suitable phrase to the first half of each Hail Mary to help you concentrate on each mystery. It may be the phrase provided in this text or one or more chosen from the biblical passage.
4. The last part of the Hail Mary may be added to each bead or at the final repetition of the Hail Mary in each decade.
5. Recite the Gloria Patri after each ten Hail Marys.
6. Say the prayer that completes each decade.
7. Pray the Marian anthem at the conclusion of each set of mysteries.

Many Catholics recite five decades of the Rosary each day; others try to pray the twenty mysteries in the course of a week. Beginners often try just one or two decades a day: quality over quantity!

Here is the weekly pattern for those who recite five decades of the Rosary each day:

1. Joyful Mysteries: Monday and Saturday
2. Luminous Mysteries: Thursday
3. Sorrowful Mysteries: Tuesday and Friday
4. Glorious Mysteries: Wednesday and Sunday

Pope John Paul II on the Most Holy Rosary

The Rosary of the Virgin Mary . . . is a prayer loved by countless saints and encouraged by the Magisterium. Simple yet profound, it still remains, at the dawn of this third millennium, a prayer of great significance, destined to bring forth a harvest of holiness. It blends easily into the journey of the Christian life, which after two thousand years has lost none of the freshness of its beginnings and feels drawn by the Spirit of God to "set out into the deep" (Luke 5:4) in order once more to proclaim, and even cry out, before the world that Jesus Christ is Lord and Savior, "the way, the truth, and the life" (John 14:6), "the goal of human history and the point on which the human desires of history and civilization turn" (Gaudium et Spes, 45).

The Rosary, though clearly Marian in character, is at heart a Christocentric prayer. In the sobriety of its elements, it has all the depth of the Gospel message in its entirety, of which it can be said to be a compendium (Pope Paul VI, Marialis Cultus, February 2, 1974, 42).

It is an echo of the prayer of Mary, her perennial Magnificat for the work of the redemptive Incarnation which began in her virginal womb.

With the Rosary, the Christian people sit at the school of Mary, and are led to contemplate the beauty on the face of Christ and to experience the depths of his love. Through the Rosary the faithful receive abundant grace, as though from the very hands of the Mother of the Redeemer.

Pope John Paul II (1920–2005)[117]

The Joyful Mysteries

1. Gabriel Brings the Message to Mary

The angel said to her, "Do not be afraid, Mary, for you have found favor with God. And now you will conceive in your womb and bear a son, and you will name him Jesus. He will be great, and will be called the Son of the Most High and the Lord God will give him the throne of his ancestor David. He will reign over the house of Jacob forever, and of his kingdom there will be no end." Then Mary said, "Here am I, the servant of the Lord; let it be with me according to your word." Luke 1:30–33, 38

THE LORD'S PRAYER

Hail, Mary, . . . the fruit of your womb, JESUS, *who was conceived at the message of an angel.*

GLORIA PATRI

Glory to the Father, and to the Son, and to the
Holy Spirit:

AS IT WAS IN THE BEGINNING, IS NOW, AND WILL
BE FOR EVER. AMEN.

PRAYER

Jesus, Word of God,
conceived in the Virgin's womb
at the message of an angel:
As we worship you in the Blessed Sacrament of
the Altar,
your continuing presence among us until the end
of the age,
may we profit by the prayers of your holy Mother
and of all the saints in glory,
now and for ever.
~AMEN.

2. Mary Visits her Cousin Elizabeth

Mary set out and went with haste to a Judean
town in the hill country, where she entered the
house of Zechariah and greeted Elizabeth. When
Elizabeth heard Mary's greeting, the child leaped
in her womb. And Elizabeth was filled with
the Holy Spirit and exclaimed with a loud cry,
"Blessed are you among women, and blessed is the
fruit of your womb." Luke 1:39–42

Hail, Mary, . . . JESUS, *who caused John to leap for
joy in his mother's womb.*

Father of all,
Mary carried the divine Child in her womb
into the home of Zachary and Elizabeth
and sanctified the child John in his mother's
       womb.
May the Virgin Mary draw us to visit Jesus
in the Blessed Sacrament of the Altar
and cause us to leap for joy
because of his continuing Presence among us
in the holy tabernacles of our churches.
We ask this through the same Christ our Lord.
~AMEN.

3. Jesus Is Born in Bethlehem of Judea

When the angels had left them and gone into
heaven, the shepherds said to one another, "Let
us go now to Bethlehem and see this thing that
has taken place, which the Lord has made known
to us." So they went with haste and found Mary
and Joseph, and the child lying in a manger.
Luke 2:15–16

Hail, Mary, . . . JESUS, *who is the Messiah, the*
     Lord, born in the city of David.

PRAYER
Abba, dear Father,
your gift to the world was the Word made flesh,
born in Bethlehem, "the House of Bread."

May he be reborn in every person who adores him
in the tabernacle of his Real Presence,
   our house of bread.
We ask this through Christ our Lord.
~AMEN.

4. Mary and Joseph Present Jesus in the Temple

Guided by the Spirit, Simeon came into the
temple; and when the parents brought in the
child Jesus, to do for him what was customary
under the law, Simeon took him into his arms,
and praised God, saying, "Master, now you are
dismissing your servant in peace, according to
your word." Luke 2:27–29

Hail, Mary, . . . JESUS, *a light for revelation to the
   Gentiles and for glory to your people Israel.*

PRAYER

Giver of all good gifts,
old Simeon and Anna rejoiced
as Mary and Joseph presented your Son
in the temple of Jerusalem.
May we enter into their joy as we worship you
in the Blessed Sacrament of the Altar
and present ourselves to your service,
now and for ever.
~AMEN.

5. Mary and Joseph Discover Jesus in the Temple

After three days they found him in the temple, sitting among the teachers, listening to them and asking them questions. He said to them, "Why were you searching for me? Did you not know that I must be in my Father's house?" Then he went down with them and came to Nazareth, and was obedient to them. His mother treasured all these things in her heart. Luke 2:46, 49–51

Hail, Mary, . . . JESUS, *who had to be in his Father's house and about his Father's business.*

PRAYER
Lord God of Israel,
you revealed to Mary and Joseph
the true calling of their dear Son
when they found him in his Father's house.
As we draw near to Jesus in the tabernacle,
may our devoted worship reveal to us
the call of God in our own hearts.
We ask this through Christ our Lord.
~AMEN.

ALMA REDEMPTORIS MATER
Mother of Christ, our hope, our patroness, *
STAR OF THE SEA, OUR BEACON IN DISTRESS,
GUIDE TO THE SHORES OF EVERLASTING DAY
GOD'S HOLY PEOPLE ON THEIR PILGRIM WAY.

Virgin, in you God made his dwelling place;
Mother of all the living, full of grace,
blessed are you: God's word you did believe;
"Yes" on your lips undid the "No" of Eve.

Daughter of God, who bore his holy One,
dearest of all to Christ, your loving Son,
show us his face, O Mother, as on earth,
loving us all, you gave our Savior birth.[118]

The Luminous Mysteries

1. John Baptizes Jesus in the Jordan

Now when all the people were baptized, and when
Jesus also had been baptized and was praying, the
heaven was opened, and the Holy Spirit descended
on him in bodily form like a dove. And a voice
came from heaven, "You are my Son, the Beloved;
with you I am well pleased." Luke 3:21–22

THE LORD'S PRAYER

Hail, Mary, . . . the fruit of your womb, Jesus, *the
Lamb of God who takes away the sins of the
world.*

GLORIA PATRI

Glory to the Father, and to the Son, and to the
Holy Spirit:
as it was in the beginning, is now, and will
be for ever. Amen.

PRAYER

Father in heaven,
when the Spirit fell on Jesus
at his baptism in the Jordan River,
you revealed him as your beloved and only Son.
Open our hearts to the same Jesus
in the Blessed Sacrament of the Altar
and make us be true adorers of his Presence,
now and for ever.
~Amen.

2. Mary and Jesus at the Wedding Feast of Cana

There was a wedding in Cana of Galilee, and the mother of Jesus was there. Jesus and his disciples had also been invited to the wedding. When the wine ran short, the mother of Jesus said to him, "They have no wine." Jesus said to the servants, "Fill the jars with water. Now draw some out, and take it to the chief steward." The steward called to the bridegroom, "You have kept the good wine until now." Jesus did this, the first of his signs, in Cana of Galilee, and revealed his glory; and his disciples believed in him. John 2:1–3, 7–8, 10–11

Hail, Mary, . . . Jesus, *who revealed his glory in Cana of Galilee; and his disciples believed in him.*

PRAYER

Lord and Savior of the world,
by Mary's intervention
you changed water into wine
and lavished it on the wedding party of Cana.
By the loving intercession of Mary,
draw us closer to your divine Presence
that flows from the tabernacle into our waiting
     hearts.
Your reign is a reign for all ages.
~AMEN.

3. Jesus Announces the Reign of God

Jesus went throughout Galilee, teaching in their
synagogues and proclaiming the good news of
the kingdom and curing every disease and every
sickness among the people. So his fame spread
throughout all Syria, and they brought to him
all the sick, and those who were afflicted with
various diseases and pains, demoniacs, epileptics,
and paralytics, and he cured them. And great
crowds followed him from Galilee, the Decapolis,
Jerusalem, Judea, and from beyond the Jordan.
Matthew 4:23–25

Hail, Mary, . . . JESUS, *who began to preach in their
    synagogues and was praised by everyone.*

Heavenly Father,
during his public life in Galilee and Judea,
your dear Son went about doing good
and preaching the coming reign of God.
May we listen to him with open ears
as we focus our attention on his personal Presence
in the Blessed Sacrament of the Altar.
We ask this through the same Christ our Lord.
~AMEN.

4. Jesus Is Transfigured on Mount Tabor

Jesus took with him Peter and James and his
brother John and led them up a high mountain by
themselves. And he was transfigured before them,
and his face shone like the sun, and his clothes
became dazzling white. Suddenly there appeared
to them Moses and Elijah, talking with him. . . .
a bright cloud overshadowed them, and from the
cloud a voice said, "This is my Son, the Beloved;
with him I am well pleased. Listen to him!" When
the disciples heard this, they fell to the ground
and were overcome by fear. Matthew 17:1–3, 5–6

Hail, Mary, . . . JESUS, *who was transfigured before
his disciples on the holy mountain.*

PRAYER

Lord Jesus, transfigured before your disciples
on Tabor, the holy mountain,
you revealed your divine nature to them
and all that you were to accomplish at Jerusalem.
Beloved Son of the Father,
fix our hearts on your divine Presence
in the Blessed Sacrament of the Altar
and make us rejoice in the Mystery of Faith,
now and for ever.
~Amen.

5. The Lord's Supper

The Lord Jesus on the night when he was betrayed
took a loaf of bread, and when he had given
thanks, he broke it and said, "This is my body
that is broken for you. Do this in remembrance of
me." In the same way he took the cup also, after
supper, saying, "This cup is the new covenant in
my blood. Do this, as often as you drink it, in
remembrance of me." 1 Corinthians 11:23–25

Hail, Mary, . . . JESUS, *who left us a share in his
precious body and his priceless blood.*

PRAYER

Holy Father of our Savior,
you had Jesus fulfill the Old Law
and bring it to perfection in the New Law.
In remembrance of him,
may we feed on his broken body

and drink his precious blood
of the new and everlasting covenant,
now and for ever.
~Amen.

Sub tuum praesidium
We turn to you for protection, *
Holy Mother of God.
Listen to our prayers
and help us in our needs.
Save us from every danger,
glorious and blessed Virgin.[119]

The Sorrowful Mysteries

1. The Agony of Jesus in the Garden of Gethsemane

When they had sung the hymn [at the end of the last supper], they went out to the Mount of Olives. And Jesus said to them, "You will all become deserters; for it is written, 'I will strike the shepherd and the sheep will be scattered.' But after I am raised up, I will go before you to Galilee." Peter said to him, "Even though all become deserters, I will not." Jesus said to him, "Truly I tell you, this day, this very night, before the cock crows twice, you will deny me three times." But he said vehemently, "Even though I must die with you, I will not deny you." And all of them said the same. Mark 14:26–31

THE LORD'S PRAYER
Hail, Mary, . . . the fruit of your womb, JESUS, *who
was betrayed by Judas with a kiss.*

GLORIA PATRI
Glory to the Father, and to the Son, and to the
Holy Spirit:
AS IT WAS IN THE BEGINNING, IS NOW, AND WILL
BE FOR EVER. AMEN.

PRAYER
Abba, dear Father,
in the time of trial as Judas betrayed him,
his disciples deserted him,
and Simon Peter denied him,
Jesus was handed over to the wicked.
By his precious sufferings and his cruel death on
the cross,
nourish and strengthen us from this altar
and prepare us to adore, thank, and praise
the Father, the Son, and the Holy Spirit,
now and for ever.
~AMEN.

2. Jesus is Tried, Condemned, and Flogged by Pilate
Pilate, wishing to satisfy the crowd, released
Barabbas for them; and after flogging Jesus, he
handed him over to be crucified. Mark 15:15

Hail, Mary, . . . Jesus, *who gave his back to those who struck him.*

Prayer

Lord Jesus,
you stood alone before a cruel and craven judge
who bowed to the rage of a mob,
and condemned you to the cross.
By the terrible flogging that readied you for death,
give us the grace to adore you
personally present for us in the Blessed Sacrament
and to stand in awe of your suffering for our sake.
Your reign, O Savior, is a reign for all ages.
~Amen.

3. Jesus Is Mocked as King of the Jews

Then the soldiers of the governor took Jesus into
the governor's headquarters, and they gathered the
whole cohort around him. They stripped him and
put a scarlet robe on him, and after twisting some
thorns into a crown, they put it on his head. They
put a reed into his right hand and knelt before
him and mocked him, saying, "Hail, king of the
Jews!" They spat on him, and took the reed and
struck him on the head. Matthew 27:27–30

Hail, Mary, . . . Jesus, *a man of suffering and acquainted with grief.*

Lord Jesus,

a man of suffering and acquainted with grief,

mocked and humiliated as King of the Jews,

prepare us for the sacramental memory of your
	death

and help us to take shelter under the wings of your
	cross,

now and for ever.

~AMEN.

4. Jesus Walks the Way of the Cross

After mocking him, they stripped him of the robe,
and put his own clothes on him. Then they led
him away to crucify him.

As they went out, they came upon a man from
Cyrene named Simon; they compelled this man
to carry his cross. And when they came to a place
called Golgotha, they offered him wine to drink,
mixed with gall, but when he tasted it, he would
not drink it. Matthew 27:31–34

Hail, Mary, . . . JESUS, *who was led out to be
	crucified and tested with insult and torture.*

PRAYER

Broken and bleeding Jesus,

on the way to Golgotha

you fell again and again under the weight of the
	cross,

until Simon of Cyrene assisted you
to mount the hill of crucifixion.
Set our hearts on the terrible death that awaited
     you
and enable us to venerate the sacrament
of your passion and death set before us
on the altar of sacrifice.
Your reign is a reign for all ages.
~AMEN.

5. Jesus Dies on the Cross

When it was noon darkness came over the whole
land until three in the afternoon. At three o'clock
Jesus cried out with a loud voice, "My God, my
God, why have you forsaken me?" Then Jesus gave
a loud cry and breathed his last. And the curtain
of the temple was torn in two, from top to bottom.
Now when the centurion who stood facing him,
saw that in this way he breathed his last, he said,
"Truly this man was God's Son!" Mark 15:33–34,
37–39

Hail, Mary, . . . JESUS, *whose sacred heart was*
    pierced by a spear and poured forth blood
    and water.

PRAYER
Lord Jesus Christ, Son of the living God,
set your passion, your cross, and your death
between your judgment and our souls,

now and at the hour of our death.
In your great goodness,
grant mercy and grace to the living,
and forgiveness and rest to the dead;
to the Church and to the nations,
  peace and concord;
and to us sinners,
  life and glory without end.[121]
~AMEN.

SALVE, REGINA
Hail, holy Queen, Mother of mercy, *
HAIL, OUR LIFE, OUR SWEETNESS, AND OUR HOPE.
TO YOU WE CRY, THE CHILDREN OF EVE;
TO YOU WE SEND UP OUR SIGHS,
MOURNING AND WEEPING IN THIS LAND OF EXILE.
TURN THEN, MOST GRACIOUS ADVOCATE,
YOUR EYES OF MERCY TOWARD US;
LEAD US HOME AT LAST,
AND SHOW US THE BLESSED FRUIT OF YOUR WOMB,
    JESUS:
O CLEMENT, O LOVING, O SWEET VIRGIN MARY.[121]

The Glorious Mysteries

1. God Raises Jesus from the Dead
I handed on to you as of the first importance what
I in turn had received: that Christ died for our
sins in accordance with the scriptures, and that

he was buried, and that he was raised on the third day in accordance with the scriptures, and that he appeared to Cephas, then to the twelve. Then he appeared to five hundred brothers and sisters at one time, most of whom are still alive, though some have died. Then he appeared to James, then to all the apostles. Last of all, as to one untimely born, he appeared also to me. 1 Corinthians 15:3–8

The Lord's Prayer

Hail, Mary, . . . the fruit of your womb, Jesus,
*who delivered us from sin and death by his
mighty resurrection, alleluia!*

Gloria Patri

Glory to the Father, and to the Son, and to the
Holy Spirit:
as it was in the beginning, is now, and will
be for ever. Amen.

Prayer

Heavenly Father, Lord of life and death,
when Christ our Paschal Lamb was sacrificed,
he overcame death by his own dying
and restored us to life by his own rising.
In virtue of his life-giving Passover,
pour your Holy Spirit into our hearts,
fill us with awe and reverence
for his blessed Presence in the Sacrament of the
Altar,

and with love and compassion for our neighbor.
We ask this through Christ our Lord.
~Amen.

2. Jesus Ascends into Heaven

Now the eleven disciples went to Galilee, to the
mountain to which Jesus had directed them.
When they saw him, they worshipped him; but
some doubted. And Jesus came to them and said
to them, "All authority in heaven and earth has
been given to me. Go therefore and make disciples
of all nations, baptizing them in the name of the
Father and of the Son and of the Holy Spirit, and
teaching them to obey everything that I have
commanded you. And remember, I am with you
always, to the end of the age." Matthew 28:16–20

Hail, Mary, . . . Jesus, *who will come again in glory
to judge the living and the dead, alleluia!*

Prayer
Heavenly Father,
you raised Jesus from the dead
and made him sit in glory at your right hand.
Teach us to adore his continuing Presence
in the Blessed Sacrament of the Altar
and give us a place with him in heaven,
in the same Christ Jesus our Lord.
~Amen.

3. Pentecost: The Gift of the Spirit

When the day of Pentecost had come, they were all together in one place. And suddenly from heaven there came a sound like the rush of a violent wind, and it filled the entire house where they were sitting. Divided tongues, as of fire, appeared among them, and a tongue rested on each of them. All of them were filled with the Holy Spirit and began to speak in other languages, as the Spirit gave them the ability. Acts 2:1–4

Hail, Mary, . . . JESUS, *who invests us with power from above, alleluia!*

PRAYER
Heavenly King, Consoler, Spirit of truth,
present in all places, filling all things,
treasury of blessings and giver of life:
Come and dwell in us
as we adore you in the Eucharistic Presence,
cleanse us from every stain of sin,
and save our souls,
O gracious Lord.
~AMEN.[122]

4. Mary Falls Asleep in Death and Is Assumed into Heaven

Christ has been raised from the dead, the first fruits of those who have died. For since death

came through a human being, the resurrection
of the dead has also come through a human being;
for as all die in Adam, so all will be made alive in
Christ. 1 Corinthians 15:20–22

Hail, Mary, . . . JESUS, *who could not leave your
soul among the dead nor let your holy body
know decay, alleluia!*

PRAYER
Father in heaven,
you raised our Blessed Mother from the dead
and assumed her body and soul into glory.
By her unceasing intercession,
lead us to perpetual adoration of her dear Son
in the Blessed Sacrament of the Altar
—our heaven on earth—even to the end of time.
~AMEN.

5. Mary's Coronation and the Glory of All the Saints

A great sign appeared in heaven: a woman
clothed with the sun, with the moon under her
feet, and on her head a crown of twelve stars.
Revelation 12:1

Hail, Mary, . . . JESUS, *who raised you up and
enthroned you with all the saints in glory,
alleluia!*

PRAYER

God of all holiness,
your crowned the sinless Virgin Mary
and enthroned her with all the saints in glory.
By our constant adoration of her Son
in the Blessed Sacrament of the Altar,
may we too be led to the glory of heaven
by the enduring prayers of Mary our Queen.
We ask this through Christ our Lord.
~AMEN.

REGINA COELI

Rejoice, O Queen of heaven, alleluia! *
FOR THE SON YOU BORE, ALLELUIA!
HAS ARISEN AS HE PROMISED, ALLELUIA!
PRAY FOR US TO GOD THE FATHER, ALLELUIA![123]

The Litany of the Blessed Virgin is often prayed to complete the full Rosary (see pages 240-242).

May the divine assistance remain always with us, and may the souls of the faithful departed † rest in peace and rise to glory.
~AMEN.

Notes

1. Robert Sokolowski, *Eucharistic Presence* (Washington, DC: Catholic University of America Press, 1993), 96.
2. Pope John Paul II (1920–2005), *Ecclesia de Eucharistia* (April 17, 2003), # 9.
3. The *Didache* (Teaching of the Twelve Apostles), section 14, Syria or Asia Minor; late first century, trans. Herbert A. Musurillo, SJ, in *The Fathers of the Primitive Church* (NY: New American Library, 1966), 61.
4. Justin Martyr (ca. 100–ca. 165), *First Apology* 67, ed. Cyril C. Richardson, *Early Christian Fathers* (New York: Macmillan, 1970), 287.
5. St. Thomas Aquinas (1225–1274), *Opusculum 57, Immensa divinae largitatis,* a homily for the Feast of Corpus Christi, translated by William George Storey.
6. St. Thomas Aquinas (1225–1274), *Pange lingua gloriosi,* trans. James Quinn, SJ, *Praise for All Seasons* (Pittsburg: Selah, 1994), 59.
7. Canons and Decrees of the Council of Trent. Thirteenth Session, chapter 1; trans. H.J. Schroeder, OP, (St. Louis, MO B. Herder, 1941), 73.
8. Blessed Angela of Foligno (ca. 1248–1309), *The Book of Angela,* Part 2, Instruction 33, trans. Paul Lachance, OFM, *Complete Works* (Mahwah, NJ: Paulist Press, 1993), 298–299.
9. *A Book of Prayers* (Washington, DC: ICEL, 1982), 5.
10. Roman Missal, from the Preface to the Feast of Corpus Christi.
11. Thomas à Kempis (ca. 1380–1471), *The Imitation of Christ,* IV, 9; ed. Harold C. Gardiner, SJ (New York: Doubleday/Image, 1963), 218–219.
12. The Bangor Antiphonary, seventh century, Ireland, trans. anon., alt.

13. Sister Benedicta Ward, SLG, *The Prayers and Meditations of St. Anselm of Canterbury* (New York, NY: Penguin Books, 1973), 100–101.

14. *A Book of Prayers* (Washington, DC: ICEL, 1982), 4.

15. Ibid., 8.

16. Ibid., 9.

17. John J. Hardon, SJ, "Jesus Help Me," by permission of the Detroit Province of the Society of Jesus.

18. *En ego, o bone Jesu,* early fourteenth century, translated by WGS.

19. *Anima Christi,* early thirteenth century, translated by WGS.

20. Abbot Louis de Blois (1506–1566), *Precationes Piae,* translated by WGS.

21. *Book of Mary* (Washington, DC: USCC, 1987), 19. The oldest known prayer to St. Mary; Coptic/Greek, late second century.

22. St. Catherine of Siena (1347–1380), Letter 229, in Augusta Theodosia Drane, *The History of St. Catherine of Siena and Her Companions* (London: Longmans, Green, and Co., 1915), 49.

23. St. Alphonsus de Liguori (1696–1787), Doctor of the Church, in *Enchiridion of Indulgences,* trans. William T. Barry, CSSR (New York: Catholic Book Publishing, 1969), 116.

24. *The Word of God Every Day 2009,* Vincenzo Paglia (Community of Sant' Egidio), 251.

25. St. Bernard of Clairvaux (1091–1153), "Hymn to Jesus," translated by Ray Palmer (1808–1887).

26. Roman Missal, Feast of Corpus Christi.

27. Pope John Paul II (1920–2005), *Ecclesia de Eucharistia* (April 17, 2003), # 61.

28. St. Francis of Assisi (1181–1226), "A Letter to the Entire Order," *Writings and Early Biographies,* ed. Marion A. Habig, fourth revised edition (Chicago: Franciscan Herald Press, 1983), 105-106. St. Anthony Messenger, 24 W. Liberty St., Cincinnati, OH 45202.

29. St. Alphonsus de Liguori (1696–1787), Doctor of the Church, *Visits to the Most Holy Sacrament,* Twenty-Third Visit, trans. Dennis Billy, CSSR (Notre Dame, IN: Ave Maria Press, 2007), 111.

30. Thomas Merton (1915–1968), *The Living Bread* (New York: Farrar, Straus & Cudahy, 1956), xix.

31. Pope John Paul II (1920–2005), *Ecclesia de Eucharistia* (Sept. 17, 2003), # 10.

32. Pope Benedict XVI (1927–), *Sacramentum Caritatis* (February 22, 2007), # 67.

33. *O sacrum convivium,* Feast of Corpus Christi, translated by WGS.

34. St. Thomas More (1478–1535), English martyr, from Michael Buckley, *The Catholic Prayer Book.* Copyright 1984. Published by Servant Books. Used with permission of St. Anthony Messenger Press, www.americancatholic.org.

35. Blessed Pope John XXlll (1881–1963), from Michael Buckley, *The Catholic Prayer Book.* Copyright 1984. Published by Servant Books. Used with permission of St. Anthony Messenger Press, www.americancatholic .org.

36. John Henry Cardinal Newman (1801–1890), *Prayers, Verses, and Devotions* (San Francisco: Ignatius Press, 2000), 335, alt.

37. Pope John Paul II (1920–2005), Letter to the Bishop of Liege on the 750th Anniversary of the Feast of Corpus Christi (May 28, 1996).

38. St. Thomas Aquinas (1225–1274), *Pange lingua gloriosi,* trans. James Quinn, SJ, *Praise for All Seasons* (Pittsburg: Selah, 1994), 59.

39. St. Cyril of Jerusalem (ca. 315–386), *Mystagogical Catecheses,* Sermon 4, 1–6, trans. Edward Yarnold, SJ, *The Awe-inspiring Rites of Initiation,* second edition (Collegeville, MN: The Liturgical Press, 1994), 86–87.

40. This litany is a composite drawn from several nineteenth- and twentieth-century sources by

Willliam G. Storey. The prayer is from the Roman
Missal, *Corpus Christi.*

41. St. Thomas Aquinas (1225–1274), *Pange lingua
    gloriosi,* trans. James Quinn, SJ, *Praise for All Seasons*
    (Pittsburg: Selah, 1994), 59.
42. St. Ambrose of Milan (ca. 339–397), *Sermons on
    the Sacraments,* Sermon 4, 13–14, trans. Edward
    Yarnold, SJ, *The Awe-Inspiring Rites of Initiation,*
    second edition (Collegeville, MN: The Liturgical
    Press, 1994), 132–133.
43. St. Thomas Aquinas (1225–1274, *Verbum supernum,*
    trans. James Quinn, SJ, *Praise for All Seasons*
    (Pittsburgh: Selah, 1994), 59.
44. St. Thomas Aquinas (1225–1274), *Immensa divinae
    largitatis,* translated by WGS.
45. St. Thomas Aquinas (1225–1274), *Sacris sollemnis,*
    trans. James Quinn, SJ, *Praise for All Seasons*
    (Pittsburgh: Selah, 1994), 60.
46. St. Cyril of Jerusalem (ca. 313–386), *Mystagogical
    Catecheses,* Sermon 4, 9, trans. Edward Yarnold, SJ,
    The Awe-Inspiring Rites of Initiation, second edition
    (Collegeville, MN: The Liturgical Press, 1994), 89.
47. *Ubi caritas est vera,* trans. James Quinn, SJ, *Praise
    for All Seasons* (Pittsburgh: Selah, 1994), 62.
48. St. Cyril of Jerusalem (ca. 313–386), *Mystagogical
    Treatise,* Sermon 5, 21, trans. Edward Yarnold, SJ,
    The Awe-Inspiring Rites of Initiation, second edition
    (Collegeville, MN: The Liturgical Press, 1994), 96.
49. St. Thomas Aquinas (1225–1274), *Lauda Sion
    Salvatorem,* trans. James Quinn, SJ, *Praise for All
    Seasons* (Pittsburgh: Selah, 1994), 67.
50. St. John Chrysostom (ca. 347–407), *Baptismal
    Homilies,* Homily 2, 27, trans. Edward Yarnold, SJ,
    The Awe-Inspiring Rites of Initiation, second edition
    (Collegeville, MN: The Liturgical Press, 1994),
    162–163.
51. James Quinn, SJ, *Praise for All Seasons* (Pittsburgh:
    Selah, 1994), 61.

52. Theodore of Mopsuestia (ca. 350–428), *Baptismal Homilies*, Homily 4, 15, trans. Edward Yarnold, SJ, *The Awe-Inspiring Rites of Initiation*, second edition (Collegeville, MN: The Liturgical Press, 1994), 209.

53. Pope Benedict XVI (1927–), *Sacramentus Caritatis* (February 22, 2007), # 66.

54 *Te Deum laudamus*, St. Nicetas of Remesiana (ca. 335–ca. 414). ELLC.

55. James Quinn, SJ, *Praise for All Seasons*, (Pittsburgh: Selah, 1994), 61.

56. Roman Missal, Feast of Corpus Christi.

57. Liturgy of St. James, translated by Gerard Moultrie (1829–1885).

58. Roman Missal, Feast of Corpus Christi.

59. *Adoro te devote*, attributed to St. Thomas Aquinas (1225–1274), trans. James Quinn, SJ, *Praise for All Seasons* (Pittsburgh: Selah, 1994), 63.

60. Stanbrook Abbey Hymnal © 1974 and 1995, Callow End, Worcester WR2 4TD.

61. *Tantum Ergo*. These are the last two verses of the hymn *Pange lingua gloriosi*, St. Thomas Aquinas (1225–1274), in trans. James Quinn, SJ, *Praise for All Seasons* (Pittsburgh: Selah, 1994), 59.

62. Pope John Paul II (1920–2005), *Dominicae Cenae*, no. 3, 1980.

63. St. Bernard of Clairvaux (1091–1153), translated by Ray Palmer (1808–1887).

64. "Act of Dedication to Christ the King," was originally written by Pope Leo XIII (1810–1903) for the feast of the Sacred Heart of Jesus. In 1925 Pope Pius XI (1857–1939) transferred it the new feast of Christ the King. It is suitable for many other occasions and especially for Holy Hours.

65. St. Bonaventure (1217–1274), *Lignum Vitae*, # 30, translated by WGS from the Breviarium Romanum, in *festo Sacratissimi Cordis Jesu* (Ratisbonae: F. Pustet, 1952), 367.

66. Stanbrook Abbey Hymnal © 1974 and 1995, Callow End, Worcester WR2 4TD.

67. Roman Missal, Feast of the Sacred Heart, alt. prayer.

68. St. Leo the Great (✝ 461), *Homily on the Lord's Ascension*, translated by WGS.

69. James Quinn, SJ, *Praise for All Seasons,* (Pittsburgh: Selah, 1994), 1.

70. From the O antiphons of the Roman Liturgy of Advent, translated by WGS.

71. Roman Missal, alt. prayer, First Sunday of Advent.

72. Roman Missal, alt. prayer, Fourth Sunday of Advent.

73. Blessed Julian of Norwich (ca. 1342–1423), *Showings,* chapter 4, trans. Edmund Colledge, OSA and James Walsh, SJ (New York: Paulist Press, 1978), 131.

74. Byzantine Christmas, translated by WGS.

75. Paraphrase of Isaiah 9:2–8 by John Morison, *Scottish Translations and Paraphrases,* 1781, alt.

76. Roman Missal, December 24, translated by WGS.

77. Roman Missal, January 1.

78. Roman Missal, January 1, alternate opening prayer.

79. Roman Missal, Baptism.

80. Attributed to St. Gregory the Great (540–604), trans. James Quinn, SJ, *Praise for All Seasons* (Pittsburgh: Selah, 1995), 11.

81. St. Leo the Great (✝ 461), *Sermon 39 on Lent,*trans. Sr. Anne Field, OSB, *The Binding of the Strong Man* (Ann Arbor, MI: Word of Life, 1976), 57.

82. Aelred-Seton Shanley, *Hymns for Morning and Evening Prayer* (Chicago: LTP, 1999), # 51.

83. *Ad cenam Agni providi,* St. Nicetas of Remesiana (ca.335–ca.414); Latin, late fourth century, translated by Robert Campbell (1814–1868), alt.

84. *Te Deumi laudamus,* St. Nicetas of Remesiana, ELLC.

85. "Easter Litany" text from a twelfth-century Latin manuscript, translated by WGS.

86. After St. Gregory the Great (ca. 540–604), Homily 29; *Breviarium Romanum,* Feria V in Octava Ascensionis; translated by WGS.

87. James Quinn, SJ, *Praise for All Seasons* (Piitsburgh: Selah, 1994), 68.

88. Roman Missal, alternate prayer.

89. Attributed to Thomas à Kempis (ca. 1380–1471), translated by John Mason Neale (1851).

90. St. Gertrude the Great (1256–1302), *The Herald of God's Loving-Kindness,* trans. Alexandra Barratt, The Cistercian Fathers Series 35 (Kalamazoo: Cistercian Publications, 1991), 109.

91. Saint Augustine of Hippo (354–430), *Directory of Popular Piety,* # 168.

92. *Quicumque certum quaeritis,* eighteenth century, translated by Edward Caswall (1814–1878), alt.

93. St. Catherine of Siena (1347–1380), Letter 27, trans. Suzanne Noffke, OP, Medieval & Renaissance Texts and Studies 52 (Binghamton, NY: 1988), 96–97.

94. Galatians 6:14, Isaac Watts (1674–1748).

95. Approved by Pope Leo XIII (1810–1903) for use throughout the world. *A Book of Prayers* (Washington, DC: ICEL, 1982), 21–23.

96. Many of the invocations in this litany can be traced to the seventeenth century. Approved by Pope Leo XIII (1810–1903). *A Book of Prayers* (Washington, DC: ICEL, 1982), 24–25.

97. Approved by Blessed Pope John XXIII (1881–1963) for the universal Church on February 24, 1960. *A Book of Prayers* (Washington, DC: ICEL, 1982), 26–27.

98. Adapted from a litany composed by Pope Pius VI (1775–1799).

99. *Byzantine Daily Worship,* ed. and trans. Archbishop Joseph Raya and Baron Jose de Vinck (Alleluia Press, 1969/1995), 989–990.

100. A Marian litany containing some of these invocations was in use in the twelfth century. It was recorded in its present form (apart from a few additions by recent popes) at Loreto in 1558 and approved by Sixtus V

Notes **289**

(1521–1590). *A Book of Prayers* (Washington, DC: ICEL, 1982), 28–29.

101. Approved by Blessed Pope Pius X (1835–1914). *A Book of Prayers* (Washington, DC: ICEL, 1982), 30–31.

102. Pope John Paul II (1920–2005), Allocution to the 45th International Eucharistic Congress (Seville, 1993), 7.

103. Pope John Paul II (1920–2005), *Ecclesia de Eucharistia* (September 17, 2003), # 62.

104. Prayer from a devotion to the Virgin Mary by St. Bernardine of Siena (1380–1444), translated and altered by WGS.

105. Pope Paul VI (1897–1978), *Marialis Cultus* (Feb. 2, 1974), 15, 13.

106. *A Book of Prayers* (Washington, DC: ICEL, 1982), 35.

107. Anonymous, fourteenth century, Middle English; translated by Dolores Warwick Frese, professor of English, the University of Notre Dame. Used with permission.

108. Blessed Guerric of Igny († 1157), *The Christmas Sermons of Blessed Guerric of Igny*, Sermon 5, translated by Sister Rose of Lima (The Abbey of Gethsemani, 1959), 60.

109. St. Francis of Assisi (1181–1226), *Writings and Early Biographies*, ed. Marion A. Habig, fourth revised edition (Chicago: Franciscan Herald Press, 1983), 135–136.St. Anthony Messenger, 24 W. Liberty St., Cincinnati, OH 45202.

110. St. Francis of Assisi (1181–1226), "The Office of the Passion," in *Writings and Early Biographies*, ed. Marion A. Habig, fourth revised edition (Chicago: Franciscan Herald Press, 1983), 142. St. Anthony Messenger, 24 W. Liberty St., Cincinnati, OH 45202.

111. A sixteenth-century abridgement of a fifteenth-century prayer, much popularized by Pere Claude Bernard (1588–1641); *Book of Prayers* (Washington, DC: ICEL, 1982), 34.

112. *Salve Regina,* eleventh century, trans. James Quinn, SJ, *Praise for All Seasons* (Pittsburgh: Selah, 1994), 96.
113. *A Book of Prayers* (Washington, DC: ICEL, 1982), 34.
114. Roman Missal, Feast of Our Lady of Guadalupe, December 12.
115. Translated from several Latin texts of the twelfth and thirteenth centuries by WGS.
116. Pope John Paul II (1920–2005), *Rosarium Virginis Mariae* (October 16, 2002).
117. Pope John Paul II (1920–2005), *Rosarium Virginis Mariae* (October 16, 2002), 1.
118. *Alma Redemptoris Mater,* trans. James Quinn, SJ, *Praise for All Seasons* (Pittsburgh: Selah Publ. Co., 1994), 97.
119. *Sub tuum praesidium,* Coptic/Greek, late second century; in *A Book of Prayers* (Washington, DC: ICEL, 1982), 35.
120. *English Prymer,* ca. 1425; translated by WGS.
121. Latin antiphon, eleventh century; in *A Book of Prayers* (Washington, DC: ICEL, 1982), 34.
122. Adapted from the Byzantine Liturgy.
123. Latin antiphon, twelfth century; translated by WGS.

Acknowledgments

Thirty-six brief Scriptural quotations (128 verses) are taken from the *New Revised Standard Version of the Bible* © 1989, Division of Christian Education of the National Council of Churches of Christ in the USA and are used by permission. All rights reserved. NRSV.

Six brief quotations (37 verses) are taken from the *New American Bible with the Revised Psalms*. Nashville: Thomas Nelson, 1987. NAB

Four brief quotations (20 verses) are taken from the *Good News Bible, Today's English Version*. New York: The American Bible Society, 1992. TEV

Unless otherwise noted, all psalms are taken from *Psalms for Prayer and Worship: A Complete Liturgical Psalter* by John Holbert et al. Nashville: Abingdon Press, 1992.

The Gospel Canticles of Zachary, Mary, and Simeon, the Te Deum, the Gloria in Excelsis, the Gloria Patri, and the Lord's Prayer are from *Praying Together: English Language Liturgical Consultation*. Nashville: Abingdon Press, 1988. ELLC.

Ten prayers from the English translation of *The Roman Missal* © 1973 and *A Book of Prayers* © 1973, by permission of the International Committee on English in the Liturgy, Inc. ICEL. All rights reserved.

Seven hymns from James Quinn, SJ, *Prayer for All Seasons*, Pittsburgh, PA: 1994.

Six excerpts from Edward Yarnold, SJ, *The Awe–Inspiring Rites of Initiation*, second edition, 1994, 2001, 2006. This edition published under license from T & T Clark, Ltd by Liturgical Press, Collegeville, MN. Used with permission.

One hymn reprinted from *Hymns for Morning and Evening Prayer* by Aelred-Seton Shanley © 1999. Archdiocese of Chicago: Liturgy Training Publications, 3949 South Racine

Ave. Chicago, IL, 60609. 1-800-933-1800. All rights reserved.
Used with permission.

Two hymns from the *Stanbrook Hymnal* © 1974 and 1995.
By permission of Stanbrook Abbey, Callow End, Worcester,
UK WR2 4TD

One excerpt from St. Leo the Great, trans. Sr. Anne
Field, OSB, *The Binding of the Strong Man*. Ann Arbor:
Word of Life, 1976.

One excerpt from *The Letters of St. Catherine of Siena*,
translated by Suzanne Noffke. MRTS Volume 52.
Binghamton, NY, 1998. Copyright Board of Regents for
Arizona State University. Reprinted with permission.

One excerpt from *Julian of Norwich: Showings*, translated
by Edmund Colledge, OSA, and James Walsh, SJ. Copyright
© 1978 by the Missionary Society of St. Paul in the State of
New York, Paulist Press. Inc., Mahwah, NJ. Reprinted by
permission of Paulist Press, Inc. www.paulistpress.com

One excerpt from *Angela of Foligno: Complete Works*, translated by Paul Lachance, OFM, Copyright © 1993 by Paul
Lachance, OFM. Paulist Press. Inc., Mahwah, NJ. Reprinted
by permission of Paulist Press, Inc. www.paulistpress.com

Three excerpts taken from *St. Francis of Assisi: Omnibus of
Sources*, volume 1, Copyright © 1991, edited by Marion A.
Habig. Reprinted with permission of St. Anthony Messenger
Press, 28 West Liberty St., Cincinnati, OH 45202

One excerpt from Guerric of Igny, *The Christmas Sermons*,
translated Sr. Rose of Lima. Copyright © Abbey of
Gethsemani. By permission of Abbot Elias Dietz, OCSO.

Excerpt from the *Imitation of Christ* by Thomas à Kempis,
translated by Harold C. Gardiner, copyright © 1955 by
Doubleday, a division of Random House, Inc. Used by permission of Doubleday, a division of Random House, Inc.

Excerpt from Alexandra Barratt, *The Herald of God's Loving
Kindness*, Cistercian Fathers Series 35. © 1991. Cistercian

Publications. Used with permission of the Liturgical Press, Collegeville, MN.

One prayer by St. Anselm of Canterbury from Benedicta Ward, SLG. *The Prayers and Meditations of St. Anselm* © 1973. New York: Penguin Group (USA), Inc.

One excerpt from *Visits to the Most Holy Sacrament and to Most Holy Mary*, translated by Dennis Billy, C.Ss.R. Copyright © 2007 by Ave Maria Press, Inc. P.O. Box 428, Notre Dame, IN 46556. www.avemariapress.com. Used by permission of the publisher.

One prayer from Vincenzo Paglia, *The Word of God Every Day*, Community of Sant'Egidio, 2009. By permission of the New York Community.

An Act of Spiritual Communion by St. Alphonsus of Liguori from the *Enchiridion of Indulgences*, Totowa, NJ: Catholic Book Publishing Corp., 1969.

One prayer of John Henry Newman, *Prayers, Verses, and Devotions*, 2nd edition, London Longmans, Green, and Co., 1893.

One prayer by St. Thomas More and a second by Pope John XXIII. Taken from Msgr. Michael Buckley, *The Catholic Prayer Book*, edited by Tony Castle. Published by Servant Books, copyright © 1986, and available at www.AmericanCatholic.org

One excerpt from Justin Martyr, *First Apology*, ed. Cyril Richardson, Early Christian Fathers. New York: Macmillan, 1970.

One excerpt from Thomas Merton, *The Living Bread*. New York: Farrar, Straus and Cudahy, 1970.

A Litany of the Resurrection from *Byzantine Daily Worship*. Allendale, NJ: Alleluia Press, 1995.

One prayer by John A. Hardon, SJ (1914–2000). By permission of the Detroit Province of the Jesuits.

One excerpt from St. Leo the Great, sermon 39, translated by Sr. Anne Field, OSB, *The Binding of the Strong Man*, Published by Word of Life, copyright © 1976 and available at www.AmericanCatholic.org

A translation of an anonymous, fourteenth-century Middle English poem by Dolores Warwick Frese, Professor of English, The University of Notre Dame. Used by permission.

Every reasonable effort has been expended in acquiring permissions from the publishers but if there are any omissions or mistakes they will be cheerfully corrected in future printings.

About the Author

William G. Storey is professor emeritus of Liturgy and Church History at the University of Notre Dame. He has compiled, edited, and authored some of the best-loved prayer books of our time. They include *An Everyday Book of Hours, A Seasonal Book of Hours, Hail, Mary: A Marian Book of Hours, A Book of Prayer for Gay and Lesbian Christians, Mother of the Americas,* and *Day by Day: The Notre Dame Prayer Book for Students.* He resides in South Bend, Indiana.